Google Pixe User (

The Concise Step-by-Step Manual with Instructions to Quickly Setup and Master Your New Google Pixel Phones with Android 13 Tips and Tricks for Beginners and Seniors

By

Park Newman

Copyright © 2023 Park Newman

All rights reserved. No part of this book shall be reproduced, stored in a retrieval system, or transmitted by any means, electronic, mechanical, photocopying, recording, or otherwise, without written permission from the publisher. Although every precaution has been taken in the preparation of this book, the publisher and author assume no responsibility for errors or omissions. Nor is any liability assumed for damages resulting from the use of the information contained herein.

This is an independent publication and has not been authorized, sponsored, or otherwise approved by Apple Inc.

Table of Contents

Chapter One 13

   Configuring Your Pixel 13

      Sync Your Existing Phone 14

      Defer The Data Transmission 16

   Convert To Pixel Phone Data 16

      Get Your Cell Phones Ready 17

      Change To Messages 19

   Power Up Your Pixel 20

      Phone Charging Instructions 21

      Using Adaptive Charging 21

      How To Charge Your Device 21

   Switch Off/On Your Phone 22

      Modify Your Power Settings 22

      Restart Your Device 23

      Begin Again (Reboot) 23

   Incorporate A SIM Card 23

      Install A SIM Card 23

      Attach The SIM Card 24

   Join Wireless Networks 25

      Switch On And Link Up 25

      Modify Your Stored Networks 27

      Join Open Wi-Fi Hotspots 28

   Join Mobile Networks 30

      Modify Cellular Network Preferences 30

      Improve Cellular Network Stability 32

Use Any Network Provider 34
   When Your Phone Is Restricted 35
How To Use Two SIM Cards 36
   Establish Two Sim Card 36
   Modify Your Dual SIM Settings 37
   Stop Using A SIM Or disable It 38
   Dual SIM Issues, Correcting 39
Set A New Background 39
   Alter Your Wallpaper 40
   Modify The Look Of The Interface 40
   Alter The Screen Layout 40
   Apply A New Wallpaper Each Day 41
   Include Icon Sets 41

Chapter Two 42
Customize Your Home Screens 42
   Insert Into Home Menus 42
   Set Up Menus And Submenus 43
   Arrange Start Menu Icons 44
   Alter The Look Of the Start Menu 44
   Swap Out Current Applications 45
Take Charge Of The Display 46
   Adjust Your Screen's Resolution 46
   Change Your Screen's Settings 47
Contact Emergency Services 50
   Get Ready For A Crisis 50
   Call For Assistance 54

- Use The Help Of An Operator 63
- Locate Earthquake Information 64
- Sign Up For Earthquake Warnings 64

Chapter Three 66
- Use Your Pixel To Go About 66
  - Pick A Mode Of Transportation 66
  - Switch Between Windows 66
  - Shift Things Around 68
- Easily Adjust Your Pixel's Settings 69
  - Invoke Fast Preferences 70
  - Adjustable On/Off Switches 70
  - Change, Delete, Or Reposition 70
  - Adjust The Volume And Video 70
  - Manage The Sound And Video 70
- File Searching And Deletion 71
  - File Browsing And Opening 71
  - Clear Up Your Pixel's Storage 71
  - Distribute, Print, And Save 71
  - Discover New Media To Like 72
  - Put Data On A Computer 72
- Use Digital Wellbeing To Regulate 72
  - Initiate Online Health Monitoring 72
  - App-Based Time Management 73
  - Determine Your Days 73
  - Bed Down With Nighttime Mode 74
- Use Automated Driving Mode 77

5

Configure Driving Settings 77

Set A Traffic Regulation 77

Switch On/Off Driver Mode 78

Use For Contactless Payments 78

Activate Near Field Communication 78

Control Contactless Payment Applications 78

Access Your Cards And Passes 79

Blocking Of Contactless Payments 79

Stop All Contactless Transactions 79

Locate Nearby Hardware 80

Install New Equipment 80

Modify The Alert Settings 81

Repair Device Setup Issues 81

Utilize The Data Saver 81

Adjust The Data Saver Setting 81

Adjust Nighttime Display Setting 82

Automatic Phone Backdrop 82

Automatically Decrease Wallpaper 83

Set Your Display Automatically 83

Turn To Screen Grayscale Instantly 84

Modify Your Theme 84

Remotely Manage Your Pixel 85

Adjust The Motion Detection 85

Make Swift Movements 85

Alter Quick Gestures Settings 86

Motions For Problem-Solving 87

Chapter Four 88
Put In And Take Calls 88
Put In A Call 89
Take A Call Or Ignore It 89
Dial The Appropriate Numbers 90
Use Wi-Fi For Phone Calls 91
Activate Wi-Fi Calling 91
Make A Wireless Call 91
Message Retrieval Instructions 92
Message Retrieving 92
Modify Your Voicemail Settings 95
The Voicemail Alerts Are Broken 95
Modify Phone Preferences 96
The Volume & Vibration Level 96
Alter The Caller Id Display 96
Alter Your Text-Based Replies 96
Modify More Parameters 97
See & Erase Call Logs 98
View Your Phone's Call Log 98
Use Address Book 99
Get Rid Of Your Call Logs 99
Spam Blockers And Caller ID 99
Activate/Deactivate Caller ID 100
Put On The Caller ID Message 101
Report A Spammer 101
Caller Id Verification / Sharing 102

- Block & Unblock A Caller 102
  - Hide A Phone Number 102
  - Filter Out Random Numbers 103
  - Remove A Call Block 103
- Call Screening & Answering 103
  - Locations That Offer Call Screen 103
  - Prepare For Instant Call Filtering 104
  - Automatically Screen Calls 105
  - Calls Are Manually Screened 105
  - Collect Call Transcripts & Recordings 106
- Multitask & Share Applications 106
  - Insert Images Inside Images 107
  - Take Out The Overlays 107
  - Cast Your Screen 107
- Utilize Direct My Call 108
  - Verify Everything You Need 108
  - Activate / Disable Direct My Call 108
  - Distribute Your Call Logs 109

Chapter Five 110
- Learn How To Use Messages 110
  - Change Your Primary Message App 110
  - Reach Out To A Contact 110
  - Enter A Phone Number 111
  - Create A New Contact 111
  - Modify Who Receives Alerts 111
  - Reject A Connection 111

- Communicate By Text / Voice 112
  - Kick Off A Discussion 112
  - Message Someone 112
  - Leave A Voicemail 112
  - Check Out The Recorded 113
  - Send On A Message 113
  - Skim Your Text Messages 113
- Images, Videos & Audio Sharing 113
  - Sending Media 114
  - Send Movies In Messages 114
  - Verbal Communication 116
  - Send In Your Coordinates 116
- Modify Message Alerts & Preferences 116
  - Modify Worldwide Preferences 116
  - Format Text Size 117
  - Resize The Screen 117
  - Modify The Intricate Options 117
- Use Pixel's Emoji References 120
  - Needed Items 120
  - Insert Appropriate Emojis 120
  - Indicative Emojis 121

Chapter Six 122
- Use A Pixel Search Features 122
  - From Any Location 122
  - Start At The Beginning 122
- Google's Pixel App Downloads 123

Get Apps With Google Play 123

Get Third-Party Applications 124

Alter / Reset A Default Software 125

Changing The Defaults 125

Reset Apps Factory Settings 125

Alter Access Settings For Apps 126

Modify Access Levels In Apps 126

Modify Access On Data Type 127

Classes Of Authorizations 127

Disable Access 127

Join Google Apps To Your Profile 128

Definition Of Sync's Effects 128

Which Applications Share Data 128

Disable The Sync Feature 129

Sync Your Account Manually 129

Manage Your Pixel Apps 129

Erase Your Downloaded Programs 130

Turn Off The Default Applications 130

Unused Software 130

Establish A Screen Lock 131

Adjust Screen Lock Settings 131

Safeguards For Your Screen 131

Using Your Fingerprint 132

Make Use Of Fingerprints 132

Create A Fingerprint System 133

Put Your Fingerprint To Use 134

- Modify Biometrics Preferences 134
- Fix Problems With Fingerprint 135
- Face Unlocks Your Pixel 137
  - Cast Off The Lock-Up 139
  - Purge Facial Records 139
  - Face Unlock's Facial Recognition 140
- Schedule Your Pixel Phone 141
  - Don't Lock Your Phone 141
  - Stop Using The Smart Lock 141
  - Find Your Locking Choices 142
- Protect Your Electronic Gadgets 144
  - Google's Password Storage 144
  - Managing Your Passwords 145
  - Handle Requests To Remember 145
  - Control Automatic Logins 145
- Locate A Lost Gadget 146
  - Locate Your Gadgets 146
  - Recover A Misplaced Pixel Phone 147
  - Remotely Locate A Device 148
- Wireless Charge Your Devices 149
  - Power For Charging 150
  - Activate Rapid Charging 150
  - Display Stand Requirements 151
  - Create A Stand For Your Pixel 151
  - Pixel Stand LED Patterns 152
  - Get Services Of Google Assistant 153

- Modify Charging Settings 154
- Modify Screen Brightness 155
- Repair Your Pixel Stand 156

Chapter Seven 158
- Manage Pixel Phone Alerts 158
  - Make Use Of Alerts 158
  - Pick Your Method Of Alert 159
  - Decide Whether To Be Notified 161
  - Set The Bubble Intensity 161
  - Manage How Alerts Appear 162
  - Display Private Information 162
- Reduce Distractions 162
  - Quickly Toggle Interruptions 163
  - Modify Your Alert Preferences 163
  - Automatically Halt Disruptions 165
- Engage With Your Applications 165
  - Needed Items 166
  - The Process Of Nearby 166

Chapter One
Configuring Your Pixel

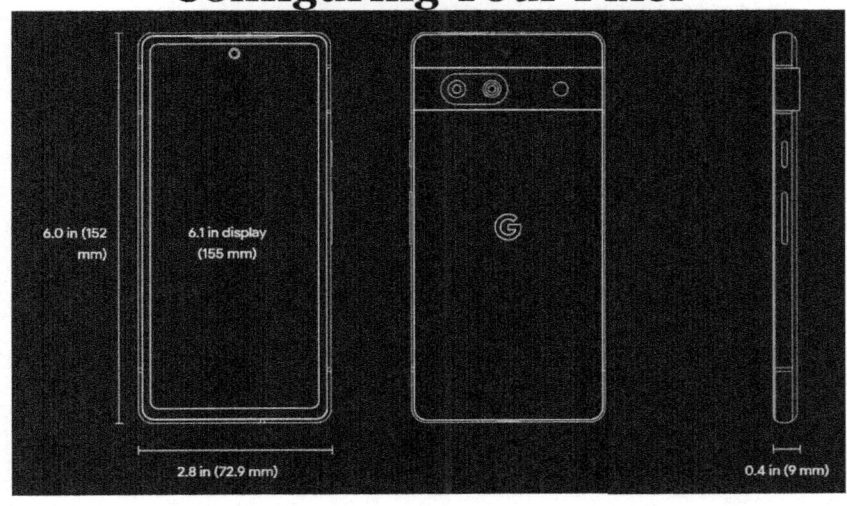

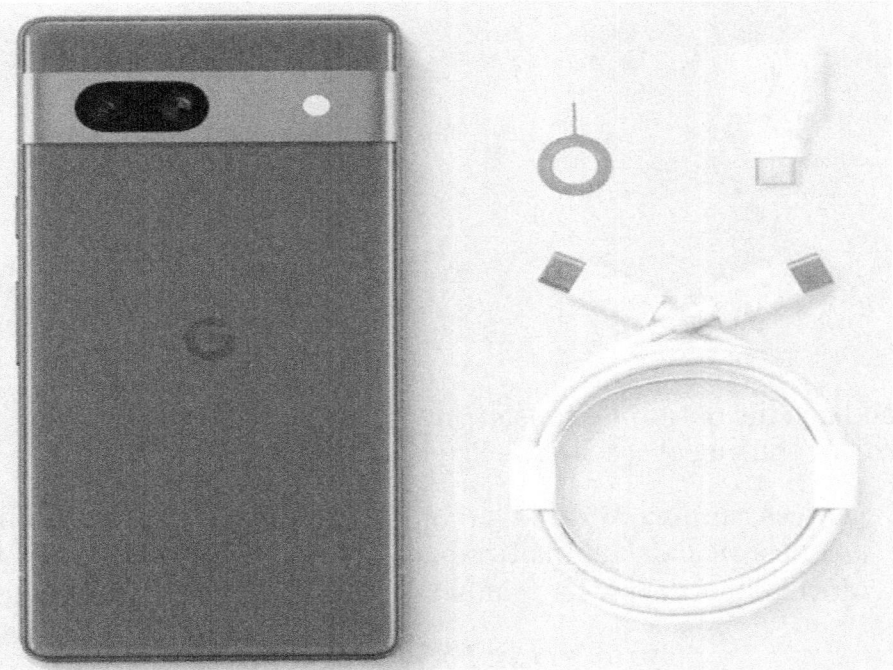

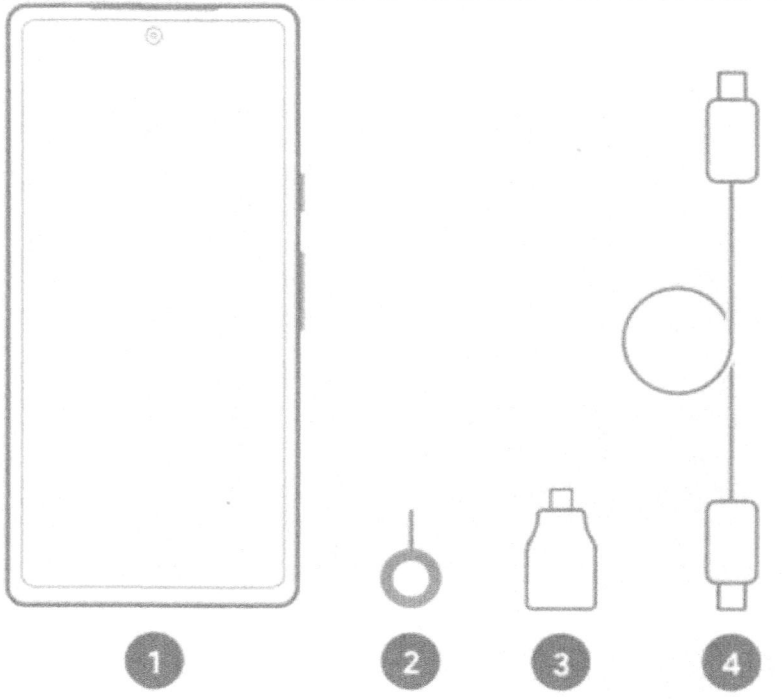

1. Pixel phone
2. SIM tool
3. Quick Switch Adapter
4. 1 m USB-C to USB-C cable (USB 2.0)
5. Support Card

You have the option of transferring data from your old phone to the Pixel or starting over with the Pixel.

- Devices running Android 5.0 or later, or iOS 8.0 or later, will be able to sync data automatically.
- Most systems allow for manual data transmission from phones.

Sync Your Existing Phone

You may sync your existing phone with a new one.

When you first power on your phone, follow the on-screen prompts to transfer data.

If you fail to complete the initial setup or data transfer:

- Your Pixel will send you a "Pixel setup isn't done" alert in a few minutes. Select Close to close the setup.
- Try launching the Settings app every day for a week. Tap Finish setup at the very top.
- You may always factory reset your phone after a period. However, doing so will delete all of your information. Figure out how to return to the defaults.

As seen on an Android device

In the beginning

1. Get a nano SIM card from your cell provider if you don't already have one.
   An eSIM may be used by your Pixel phone if it is compatible with your mobile service provider. Contact your service provider for further information.
2. Locate a cable, such as a charger, that is compatible with your present phone.
3. Locate your Quick Switch Adapter if your current phone or cable doesn't use USB-C. Examine the contents of the phone's packaging.

Send Over Your Files

In the beginning

1. Get a nano SIM card from your cell provider if you don't already have one.
   An eSIM may be used by your Pixel phone if it is compatible with your mobile service provider. Contact your service provider for further information.
2. Maximize the amount of information that can be sent.
3. Locate a cable, such as a charger, that is compatible with your present phone.
4. Locate the Adapter for a Fast Switch.

Send Over Your Files

From a Windows Phone 7 or BlackBerry

In the beginning

Get a nano SIM card from your cell provider if you don't already have one.

An eSIM may be used by your Pixel phone if it is compatible with your mobile service provider. Contact your service provider for further information.

Defer The Data Transmission

Turn on your Pixel phone, go to Settings, and then press Start, and then set up as new if this is your first smartphone or you just want to start again. You won't bother with the data transfer and will immediately begin customizing your new phone.

Convert To Pixel Phone Data

Information like text messages, pictures, music, calendar events, and app data may all be copied.

Products that are Pixel-copy able

Where do the various setup copies go?

While setting up, feel free to steal these:

- Data from and on apps
- Songs, pictures, and movies
- Google IDs
- Phonebook entries or SIM card information
- Instant Messages
- Generally speaking (albeit it varies by phone and Android version)
- Text message multimedia
- Background Call Logs

When you log into your Google Account on your Pixel phone, you'll see the following:

- Email
- Contacts
- Scheduled Occasions

- Information about you that Google doesn't already know is crucial: To-do lists, schedules, and Google notes you make on your Pixel phone will automatically be synced with your online Google Account storage. When you login into your Google Account on your Pixel phone, your information from both accounts is synchronized.

When setting up, what won't replicate

- Content available for download, such as PDF documents
- Files containing private media such as photos, movies, and audio
- Non-Google Play Store applications
- Information saved by applications that don't sync with Android backup
- Data from accounts outside Google Accounts
- Synchronization of non-Google calendars and contacts
- Settings on your phone (may vary by model and Android version).
- After you've put everything up, learn how to transmit some of this information.

Get Your Cell Phones Ready

Get Your New Pixel Ready For Use.
1. Get the batteries charged up on both devices.
2. Complete all available updates on your existing phone.
3. Obtain what you need.
   - A compatible cable, such as a charging cord, for your current phone model.
   - If your existing phone or cable doesn't use USB-C, you'll need a Quick Switch Adapter.
   - Unless you're utilizing Google Fi as your cell provider and an eSIM, your SIM card, and the equipment used to install SIM cards.
4. Launch Google's Pixel launcher on your Pixel phone.

Open the Pixel app.
Activate your Pixel and choose the Get Started option. You may modify the phone's language and/or accessibility features.

Put in your SIM card.
1. A SIM card must be inserted.
2. There will be a Start button there.

Connect the phones.
You can sync your old phones with your new Pixel to transfer data:

1. Online data storage
2. A cable and your old phone (preferred).
3. Access to Wi-Fi (Android version 12 or later required).

Make A Duplicate Of Your Files
Data may be restored from the cloud.

1. If you're using a Pixel phone:
   - Start the installation process by pressing the Start button.
   - Get online using a wireless network or your mobile service provider.
2. When prompted to "Copy Apps & Data," choose Next.
3. If prompted to "Use your old device," choose "Yes." You can't use that outdated phone anymore.
4. To access your backup, sign in to your Google Account as directed.

Use a cable to transfer your data from your old phone to the new one.

1. If you're using a Pixel phone:
   - Select the "Start" button.
   - Join a wireless network or a mobile service.
2. After being prompted to "Copy Apps & Data," Choose Next. Make a copy of your files.
3. If you'd like to "Use your old device," choose Next.
4. Activate your Android and login to it.
5. Connect the Android end of the charging cord to the device.
6. The other end of the cable may be plugged directly into your Pixel phone, or the Quick Switch Adapter can be used with the Pixel phone.

   Is no cable available? Some of your data may be suitable for wireless transmission.

7. Select Trust on your Android interface.
8. Your information is shown in a list on your Pixel phone.
   - All of your information may be copied with a single press on the Copy button.
   - Disable unwanted features to selectively copy data.
   - Choose Copy.
9. Your phone will be available for use after the transfer is complete.

   It may take a while for certain applications to appear once you download and install them.

Wireless data transfer (Android 12+)

To transmit data wirelessly, both your old and new Android devices must be running Android 5 or later and Android 12 or later, respectively.

1. If you're using a Pixel phone:
   - Select the "Start" button.
   - Join a wireless network or a mobile service.
2. After being prompted to "Copy Apps & Data," Choose Next. Make a copy of your files.
3. If you'd like to "Use your old device," choose Next.
4. When prompted to "Find your old phone's cable," choose No cable.
5. To dismiss the alert, choose Ok.
6. The existing phone has to be turned on and unlocked.
7. Access the new phone setup prompt on your existing device.
8. Your information will be shown on your Pixel phone.
   - All of your information may be copied with a single press on the Copy button.
   - Disable unwanted features to selectively copy data.
   - Choose Copy.
9. After the money has been sent, you may use your phone again.

Change To Messages

Messages for Android are superior to Apple's iMessage for receiving text messages on your new Android phone.

Take care not to damage your iPhone by removing the SIM card.

Before removing the SIM card from your iPhone, make sure iMessage is turned off. If you don't change the settings, your old iPhone may keep receiving SMS and MMS messages meant for your new one.

Disable iMessage

1. Select "Settings" from the iPhone's menu.
2. Select "Messages."
3. Turn off iMessage by selecting the Settings cogwheel.

Restart your chat groups.

To ensure that you continue to get messages from your iPhone-using pals, you need to create a new group chat. The new group conversation may be initiated by anybody, not just you.

Have you already taken out your iPhone's SIM card?

You should contact Apple to get your phone number deleted from iMessage if you no longer have access to your previous iPhone or have already removed the SIM card.

Power Up Your Pixel

USB-C cables are compatible with all Pixel phones. The power adapter included with certain phones, such as the Pixel 5a (5G), is optimal for charging the device.

Your Pixel 7, Pixel 7 Pro, Pixel 6, Pixel 6 Pro, or Pixel 5 may act as a wireless charging pad for other Qi-compatible devices, such as your Pixel Buds, when you set up Battery Share. You may charge a second phone or accessory by placing it on the back of your primary device.

The performance of a lithium-ion battery like the one in your Pixel phone might decrease with time and use. Some Pixel phones may make adjustments to charging to deal with device and battery temperatures to prolong battery life. This may cause a decrease in charging speed.

A fully charged battery is required for wireless charging using Battery Share. The Settings menu is where you can see how much juice you have left on your phone. Use the Battery > Battery Share menu option. Put your phone somewhere cool to avoid overheating it.

Phone Charging Instructions
1. Connect the USB-C end of the cable to your phone's bottom port.
2. Connect the opposite end of the cord to the phone's charger.
3. Put the plug of your adaptor into the wall socket.

Using Adaptive Charging
You should know that your phone may utilize Adaptive charging if you plug it in between 9 p.m. and 4 a.m. and have an alarm set at 3 a.m. to 10 a.m. Your phone won't be able to utilize this function until you enable it.

Constant overnight charging may help extend the life of your phone's battery. With adaptive charging, you may schedule your alarm to charge your phone to full capacity in time for you to use it in the morning.

Disabling Adaptive charging entails:

1. Get the phone's configurations menu going.
2. Use the Battery and Adaptive Preferences buttons.
3. Adaptive charging should be disabled.

To help you keep track, the Always On Display will read "Adaptive charging" and the estimated time until your battery is completely charged if you turn on Adaptive charging.

How To Charge Your Device
- Plug it into an electrical socket in the wall. It takes longer to charge certain devices than others, such as laptops.
- Your phone may be charged as you use it. Avoid using it while charging to maximize charging time.

Listen to the charging sound on your phone.

1. Verify that your phone's ringer is activated.
2. Launch the device's configuration menu.
3. Clicking sound, then onwards.
4. Toggle on the charging noises.
5. There will be a beep when your phone is plugged in.

You won't hear anything if your phone is muted or set to vibrate.

How to plug in and what cords to use

- USB-C cables and chargers compatible with USB 2.0 are required for Pixel phones.
- Use a USB-C to USB-A cable to charge your phone from a USB-A wall charger. This method is slower than USB-C for charging your mobile device.
- Pixel phones may be incompatible with other Android cords and chargers.
- There is no wireless charging support for the Pixel 4a (5G), Pixel 4a, Pixel 3a, Pixel 2, or Pixel (2016).

Informational Notes

- We advise taking the device to a certified service center if you need the battery removed. It is not suggested that you undertake the removal on your own.
- The AC adaptor is country/region specific.

Having problems with your Pixel phone even now?

You may ask the Pixel community on our forums for help resetting your phone if you run into any further problems.

Switch Off/On Your Phone

The top button on the right side of your phone controls the power.

Modify Your Power Settings

- If your phone is off and you want to switch it on, press and hold the Power button until the screen lights up.
- Press and hold the Power button for up to seven seconds on a Pixel 6 or later to activate the device.
- If your phone is on and you want to switch it off:

- For a few seconds, press and hold the Power button on your Pixel 5a or earlier. Then, press the Power off button on your device.
- To turn off your Pixel 6 or later device, press and hold the Power and volume up keys at the same time for several seconds. Then, press the Power off button on your device.

I recommend charging your phone before you use it.

Restart Your Device

Pressing the Power button once while the phone is on will toggle the display on and off.

The clock and other information may be seen in the dark on some Pixel phones.

Begin Again (Reboot)

1. Phone, please restart.
   - For Pixels as old as the 5a: If your phone has to be restarted, press and hold the Power button for 30 seconds.
   - Hold the Power and Volume Up keys for a few seconds to force a soft reset on Pixel 6 and later devices.
2. Click the Restart button.

Incorporate A SIM Card

An operational nano SIM card or electronic SIM may link your phone to a cellular data network. If you don't have one, you'll get a "No SIM card" alert.

Some of these instructions need Android 11 or later.

Install A SIM Card

Nano SIM cards are supported by all Pixel phones. The usage of eSIM is available on several Pixel phones.

Once you purchase a Pixel device through the Google Store:

- SIM cards are optional in the United States; however, a Verizon SIM card is included with certain phones. Your Verizon SIM card must be activated on the Verizon website.
- A SIM card is required to use your phone in other countries.

Substitute A Tiny SIM Card
- A nano SIM card may be obtained by contacting a mobile service provider.
- Instead of purchasing a whole new phone, you may just swap the SIM card with a nano SIM card.

Employ eSIM
eSIM functionality varies by device and mobile service provider. Contact your service provider for further information.

- All Pixel 4 and subsequent devices support eSIM functionality.
- Phones purchased from Verizon or in Japan will not support eSIM if they are a Pixel 3a.
- Phones purchased from US or Canadian carriers other than Sprint and Google Fi that use the Pixel 3 do not support eSIM. eSIM is not compatible with phones purchased in Australia, Taiwan, or Japan.
- Only Pixel 2 phones activated via the Google Fi service may use an eSIM.
- No Pixel phones support eSIM in 2016.

Attach The SIM Card
When your phone is turned off, attach the SIM card.

1. The SIM ejection tool is inserted into a tiny hole on the left side of the phone.
   A SIM card slot may be seen on the bottom of the Pixel 3 (2018).
2. Gently yet firmly press until the tray releases.
3. Take out the card reader and slide the nano SIM card into place.
4. Carefully replace the tray with its holder.

To restore mobile service, you may need to restart your phone. Pressing the power button for three seconds can force a phone to restart if it is already on. Finally, choose Restart from the menu.

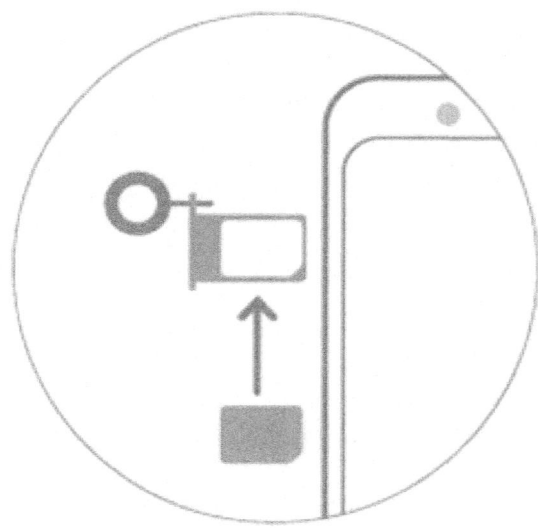

Put SIM card in

Obtain the serial number from your phone.

Pixel ID numbers such as the International Mobile Equipment Identity (IMEI) 1, IMEI 2, and EID may be required while communicating with your carrier.

Join Wireless Networks
Join wireless networks with your Pixel smartphone.

You may customize your Wi-Fi experience by changing when and how your phone connects.

With Wi-Fi enabled, your phone will connect to any previously used networks in the area. Phones may be programmed to connect to Wi-Fi automatically when they are in the range of certain networks.

Some of these instructions need Android 11 or later.

Switch On And Link Up
1. Launch the device's configuration menu.
2. Use the Network & Internet menu to go online.
3. Connect to Wi-Fi.

4. Use one of the specified networks. You will see the Lock symbol if a password is required. Once you've joined a network, the word "Connected" will appear next to its name.
   - The system has been "Saved." Your phone will connect automatically when you are in range and have Wi-Fi turned on.

The Wi-Fi menu may also be accessed by swiping down from the top of the screen.

Keep In Touch Via Alerts

When enabled, Wi-Fi alerts you to the presence of secure, public networks with which to connect. Regarding these alerts:

- The Connect button initiates a connection to the desired network.
- Select All Networks to modify your wireless preferences.
- You may disable network alerts by clearing the notification.

You may join these networks in stealth mode as well.

Evaluate the relative power of different networks. Strength

1. Launch the device's configuration menu.
2. Use the Network & Internet menu to go online.
3. Check to see whether Wi-Fi is active.
4. The Wi-Fi indicator shows how strong the network connection is. Indicating a stronger signal is a fuller icon.

Speed

1. Launch the device's configuration menu.
2. Use the Network & Internet menu to go online.
3. Check to see whether Wi-Fi is active.
4. Under the name of a public network is where you'll see the data transfer rate. As signal strength varies, so may the speed.
   - Slow: Emails and text messages may be sent and received. The images load gradually.

- OK: You may access the internet for reading, social networking, and listening/watching videos in standard definition (SD).
- Quick: most high-definition (HD) video streaming and video calls are possible.
- High-quality video streams in a short amount of time.

Turn on nearby saved networks mechanically.

1. Launch the device's configuration menu.
2. Select Internet from the menu, followed by Network Preferences.
3. Power on Activate Wi-Fi instantly. If it is required, enable Location and then enable Location services.
4. Start searching for available networks using Wi-Fi and Bluetooth.

Wi-Fi won't activate routinely if:

- Misplaced location
- Airplane mode and battery saving are both engaged.
- Tethering (sometimes known as a "hotspot") is enabled. Turning off Wi-Fi scanning

Modify Your Stored Networks

You may edit, import, export, and delete your stored networks.

Swap out a previously stored connection

1. Gets the phone's configurations menu going.
2. Select Wi-Fi from the Network and Internet menu.
   - Tap a network's name to go to that network in the list.
   - Tap the network to see its options menu.

Flushing The Network List

If the desired network is not shown but is close by, you should refresh the list.

Integrate A System

1. Launch the device's configuration menu.

2. Use the Network & Internet menu to go online.
3. Check to see whether Wi-Fi is active.
4. Add a network by swiping down to that option.
5. If prompted, provide the network's SSID and password.
6. Pick the Save option.

Give your pal your Wi-Fi password.

1. Launch the device's configuration menu.
2. Use the Network & Internet menu to go online.
3. Check to see whether Wi-Fi is active.
4. Select a connection, and then click the Share button.
5. There is a QR code on your mobile device. To join the same network as you, your buddy only has to scan the code.

Cancel saved connections

1. Gets the phone's configurations menu going.
2. Use the Network & Internet menu to go online.
3. Check to see whether Wi-Fi is active.
4. Tap and hold a favorite connection to recall it.
5. The Forget button.

Join Open Wi-Fi Hotspots
Join open Wi-Fi hotspots without a password.

OpenRoaming is a consortium of wireless Internet access points. Your Pixel phone will immediately connect to an available OpenRoaming hotspot in your area that provides free, encrypted internet access to Google users.

Facilitate OpenRoaming.

You must be in the range of an OpenRoaming network to start up OpenRoaming. After initialization, your phone will connect to any OpenRoaming networks in range.

Activate OpenRoaming on your Pixel by doing the following:

1. Launch the device's configuration menu.
2. Use the Network & Internet menu to go online.

3. When an OpenRoaming network appears in the Wi-Fi list, you may choose to connect to it.
4. Read the disclaimer that appears on the screen. Pick the Next button.
5. Select the Google ID you'd want to use.

The OpenRoaming options may be disabled or altered.

Your OpenRoaming account may be forgotten, deactivated, or swapped out at any time.

1. Launch the phone's Settings menu when connected to an OpenRoaming hotspot.
2. Use the Network & Internet menu to go online.
3. If you want to change the settings for "OpenRoaming," it's right next to it.
   - To end your connection to that hotspot entirely, choose the option to do so.
   - Select Forget to permanently disconnect from OpenRoaming.
   - OpenRoaming allows you to switch your account by going to Settings > Advanced > Subscription.

Other data, like the signal strength, frequency, and security of the active hotspot, may be found under Settings.

OpenRoaming and its operation

Google will not provide any OpenRoaming network access to your personal information.

OpenRoaming streamlines the process of connecting to open Wi-Fi networks. You won't have to manually accept the terms and conditions of each network you join. Instead, when you go from one hotspot region to another, your Pixel phone will swap networks for you automatically.

Networks that want to participate in OpenRoaming must first agree to a set of shared terms and conditions and service and security requirements. When you first start up OpenRoaming, you will be asked to agree to these standard conditions.

After you've completed the setup, your Pixel phone will provide an accepted Google credential to OpenRoaming networks. Because of this, switching between OpenRoaming hotspots on your Pixel phone is a breeze.

Join Mobile Networks

Changing your phone's mobile network settings might affect how much data your phone consumes.

Your phone may automatically connect to your carrier's fastest available data network, depending on your carrier and service package. In certain cases, a SIM card or carrier-specific settings may need to be added.

5G service is compatible with the Pixel 4a (5G) and later.

Some of these instructions need Android 11 or later.

Modify Cellular Network Preferences
1. Launch the device's configuration menu.
2. Use the SIM cards, and then connect to the network.
3. Select an option by tapping it.

The System, Advanced, and Reset options may be found in the Settings app on your phone. Wi-Fi, cellphone, and Bluetooth may all be reset thereafter.

Options for mobile network configurations

The following choices are device- and Android-specific:

- You may toggle mobile data on and off from your device.
- When you leave your service provider's coverage region, your phone might use the networks of other providers (known as "roaming").
- Utilization of App Data.
- Limitation and data warning
- The network architecture of choice: Choose from available network choices like 5G and LTE.
- Choose your preferred network provider from the available options.

- Network name or SSID: Assist your service provider in determining your phone's unique IP address and establishing a safe, encrypted connection.

Mobile network configurations with several SIM cards

If your phone accepts more than one SIM card, you may customize the settings for each SIM individually by tapping their respective tab at the top of "Mobile network settings."

Establish a primary SIM for all telephony and texting functions

1. Activate the system preferences by launching the appropriate program.
2. Select SIMs, followed by your network, under Network & internet.
3. Make the following selections for each network:
   - Data: Engage Mobile Data.
     Only one SIM card may be set as the default for data access. A notice will be sent if one has already been set up.
   - To choose your preferred method of contact, just press the Call Preference button. Then, either choose a default carrier or choose the "Ask me every time" option.
   - To set your SMS preferences, click the corresponding menu item. Then, either choose a default carrier or choose the "Ask me every time" option.

Change your SIM card before making calls

During a call, you will not receive a call on the other SIM card. It will forward calls to voicemail on the other SIM card.

The default SIM card for that use type handles the vast majority of data transfers. Exception: The SIM card in the calling phone is the conduit for all information throughout the conversation.

To make data calls using a SIM card that isn't dedicated to data use:

1. Activate the system preferences by launching the appropriate program.
2. Select SIMs after selecting Network & Internet.

3. Make sure Data is on while on a call.

Improve Cellular Network Stability

The quality and rate of a connection are not constant. Consider factors like network traffic and your physical location concerning any antennas.

If you are inside your network's service area but still experiencing a poor connection, try the following:

Examine for mistakes, updated settings, and malfunctioning components

1. Get in touch with your service provider if you get a SIM-related problem message.
    - Two SIMs may cause an error message reading "Voice unavailable" or "Voice interruptions."
2. Be careful to turn off "Airplane Mode."
    - Gets the phone's configurations menu going.
    - Use Your Network and the Web.
    - Disable the airplane setting.
3. Your network settings need to be reset.
    - Get the phone's configurations menus going.
    - Select System, then Advanced, and finally Reset.
    - Select Factory Reset to remove all wireless connections and Bluetooth settings.
4. Do a check for software updates.

Verify that your phone and carrier support the SIM card you want to use.

Verify 5G's Sluggish Connection

If you're at a location with access to 5G data, your phone's status bar will display a 5G icon. That doesn't imply you'll have access to 5G on your phone at that moment.

Here's what to do:

- Disable the battery saver. Power saving mode disables 5G.

- Only one SIM card should be used at a time. In DSDS mode, 5G cannot be used simultaneously on two different SIM cards.
- Some 5G service provider networks only cover limited regions. Ask your service provider where you may get 5G service.
- Several variants of 5G may be made available by various carrier networks. Varies in speed. Ask your service provider about the 5G options and speeds they provide.
- Mobile service, especially 5G, may be disrupted by signal barriers like buildings, walls, and even certain phone covers. Remove or relocate any obstacles you can.
- Pixel phones that support 5G automatically switch to 4G and other networks if 5G service isn't available.

Verify that it works with 5G

All major carriers support Pixel phones. However, not all phones built after the Pixel 4a (5G) are compatible with all 5G networks. Make sure your phone is compatible with your carrier's 5G network.

The specifics of the 5G service you need will depend on both the phone you use and the carrier's network. Some Verizon-compatible Pixel 4a (5G) phones are available in the United States.

How to Tell if You're on 5G with Pixel

Those in Denmark, Norway, and Sweden should check for software updates.

Problems Or Difficulties Connecting
- Customers in Denmark and Norway who use the TDC and ICE networks using a Pixel 6a, 7, or 7 Pro
- The newest software is required for 5G network connectivity.
- To implement the upgrade:
- To update your system, go to Settings > System > System Update.
- Two new Pixel phones, the 7 and 7 Pro: During the setup process, you will be requested to upgrade the phone's operating system.

- It is unclear whether or when Pixel users that use the OneCall or MyCall (Norway) networks will have access to 5G services on those networks.
- 5G availability, throughput, and performance may be conditional on the capacity and quality of the underlying operator network. The potential for varying outcomes exists. Not all regions have access to all features. Data charges may apply.

My Pixel doesn't support Wi-Fi calling.

- Wi-Fi calling capabilities may not be supported by all carriers or even all countries. There are a lot of variables that affect call quality and performance. Wi-Fi network capabilities and signal strength are examples of such elements.

Use Any Network Provider
You may use your Pixel with any network provider.

A SIM-unlocked phone may be used with any GSM network provider, not simply the one the buyer originally signed up with. Depending on where you got it, your phone might have either a SIM lock or be unlocked.

All major carriers support Pixel phones. However, not all phones built after the Pixel 4a (5G) are compatible with all 5G networks. Make sure your phone is compatible with your carrier's 5G network.

Obtain a SIM-free phone and start using it.

Your Pixel, so long as it is SIM-unlocked, may be used with any network. The Google Play Store sells only unlocked phones.

If you have a SIM-free phone, you can:

1. Purchase a Pixel phone from the Google Store with its sim card removed.
2. Get in touch with your cellphone provider.
3. Get your phone set up with their service by following their instructions.

The "Fi" icon will appear on unlocked Google Store phones until they are activated with a service provider.

When Your Phone Is Restricted

A cell carrier may restrict your phone to their SIM card for as long as two years if you buy it from them. If so, the phone will be locked to that carrier's service until either the contract expires or the vendor unlocks the SIM.

Contact your mobile service provider to explore your possibilities for unlocking your phone's SIM card before the end of your sales contract.

Resolve Difficulties Caused By A SIM Lock Removal

Your SIM may need to be refreshed if it still doesn't operate after your old carrier has removed the SIM-lock and your new carrier has verified service. A message stating "SIM card isn't supported" or "Your service can't be activated" can appear.

Simple troubleshooting techniques

1. Join a wireless network.
2. Get the most recent Android update.
3. Launch the app on your phone.
4. Enter the code: *#*#7465625#*#*.
5. Wait about two minutes until the dialer screen reappears.
6. Determine whether a mobile data connection is available.

Perform complex troubleshooting procedures

Return To Original Settings

Resetting your phone to factory settings is an option if simple troubleshooting doesn't help.

Following the deletion of all content from your phone, you may begin setting it up again by selecting the restart option and then following the on-screen prompts.

Take up with your service provider immediately.

If you have tried restoring your phone to factory settings and are still unable to connect to a mobile network, you should contact your service provider.

How To Use Two SIM Cards
Using two SIM cards on your Google Pixel

You may utilize both a traditional SIM card and an eSIM on a Pixel 3a or later Pixel phone. When making a call or sending a text message, for example, you may choose which SIM to use. The acronym DSDS refers to this feature.

If your network provider supports it, you may have two eSIM profiles active at once on your Pixel 7 or Pixel 7 Pro.

You must first insert the first SIM card before inserting a second one.

Some mobile service providers support DSDS and eSIM. If you want to know whether they're compatible with your phone, contact your service provider. You can't use two SIM cards in a Pixel 3a purchased in Japan.

Dual SIM Pixel 4a (5G) and subsequent models are compatible with 5G networks.

Establish Two Sim Card

Instructions for adding a second SIM card to your Google Pixel the procedures in this guide will not be available until Android version 11.

Make use of an electronic SIM card.

If your phone is already utilizing a SIM card but doesn't have an eSIM installed, do the following.

1. Gets the phone's configurations menu going.
2. Access the Internet and network.
3. Select "Mobile network" and press the "Add" button.
4. Use the Download a SIM option instead.
5. In response to "Use 2 SIMs?" choose Yes. Your phone will soon update.

6. Launch the Settings menu once again when your phone has completed its update.
7. To connect to a mobile network, choose Network & Internet.
8. Use your networks' call and text settings to customize your experience.

Choose "Ask me every time" when prompted to choose a network.

Double up on eSim profiles

Double your eSIM profile capacity on supported devices by:

1. Launch the device's configuration menu.
2. Select SIMs after tapping Network & Internet.
3. Tap What about a SIM card download?
4. Just do as it says.

A second SIM card may be added.

Using a phone that has an eSIM but no physical SIM card installed:

1. Just pop the SIM card in there.
2. In response to "Use 2 SIMs?" choose yes. Your phone will soon update.
3. Launch the Settings menu once again when your phone has completed its update.
4. To connect to a mobile network, choose Network & Internet.
5. Use your networks' call and text settings to customize your experience.

Choose "Ask me every time" when prompted to choose a network.

Modify Your Dual SIM Settings

Some of these instructions need Android 11 or later.

Your mobile device gives you the freedom to choose which SIM card to use for all of your communication needs. The SIM card is immediately used by your phone.

Establish a primary SIM for all telephony and texting functions

1. Activate the system preferences by launching the appropriate program.

2. Select SIMs, followed by your network, under Network & internet.
3. Make the following selections for each network:
   - Data: Engage Mobile Data.
   Only one SIM card may be set as the default for data access. A notice will be sent if one has already been set up.
   - To choose your preferred method of contact, just press the Call Preference button. Then, either choose a default carrier or choose the "Ask me every time" option.
   - To set your SMS preferences, click the corresponding menu item. Then, either choose a default carrier or choose the "Ask me every time" option.

Change your SIM card before making calls

During a call, you will not receive a call on the other SIM card. It will forward calls to voicemail on the other SIM card.

The default SIM card for that use type handles the vast majority of data transfers. Exception: The SIM card in the calling phone is the conduit for all information throughout the conversation.

To make data calls using a SIM card that isn't dedicated to data use:

1. Activate the system preferences by launching the appropriate program.
2. Select SIMs after selecting Network & Internet.
3. Make sure Data is on while on a call.

Stop Using A SIM Or disable It

Some of these instructions need Android 11 or later.

Temporarily disable a SIM card

To switch off a SIM card temporarily:

1. Launch the device's configuration menu.
2. To connect to a mobile network, choose Network & Internet.
3. To disable a specific SIM card, just choose it.
4. Select the SIM menu option.

Pixel 4a (5G) and subsequent models with dual SIM support can access 5G networks.

Remove an eSIM or make its removal password-protected.

To Remove An Esim, Delete It.
1. Launch the device's configuration menu.
2. To connect to a mobile network, choose Network & Internet.
3. To remove an eSIM, choose it from the list.
4. Select the SIM Delete option.

To Remove An Esim Card, A Password Is Required.
1. Launch the device's configuration menu.
2. Select Confirm SIM erasure by going to Settings > Security > Advanced.

Don't use a SIM card anymore.

Take it off the mobile device.

Dual SIM Issues, Correcting

Some of these instructions need Android 11 or later. Find out how to verify your Android version.

Not all SIM network configurations are compatible with one another. Whenever you get "Voice unavailable" or "Voice interruptions," it's because the networks on your two SIM cards aren't cooperating. The best place to go for support is your cell service provider.

Obtain the serial number from your phone.

Pixel ID numbers such as the International Mobile Equipment Identity (IMEI) 1, IMEI 2, and EID may be required while communicating with your carrier.

Set A New Background

The wallpapers on your Home screens and lock screens are customizable. You may utilize your photographs, as well as the preloaded, dynamic images that come with your phone.

- You'll need Android 10 or later to complete some of these procedures.
- You'll need to use your fingers to go through some of these menus.

Alter Your Wallpaper

1. Touch and hold a blank area on your phone's Home screen.
2. Select a wallpaper and a theme from the menu. If you don't see "Wallpaper & style," choose Wallpapers.
3. Select the Wallpaper menu.
   - Select "My photos" to upload a personal photo.
   - Select a group and then a picture to utilize the group's selection.
   - From the Pixel 2 on Simply choose Bloom or Living Universe and then a wallpaper to begin using a living background. If it's necessary, choose Download.
   - Only the Pixel 4: You'll need Live Wallpaper set up before you can use Motion Sense with your wallpaper. Choose wallpaper by tapping the Come Alive button, and then tap Download.
4. In the lower-right corner, choose Set wallpaper or Done.
5. Select the screen(s) you want to use as the wallpaper's primary display.

Modify The Look Of The Interface

To customize the look of your Home screen's text, icons, and background:

1. Touch and hold a blank area on your phone's Home screen.
2. Select a wallpaper and a theme from the menu.
3. Choose a basic color or a wallpaper color.
4. Pick your flavor.
5. Done or the Apply button should be tapped.

Alter The Screen Layout

On the Home screen, to change the grid size:

1. Touch and hold a blank area on your phone's Home screen.
2. Select the wallpaper and a theme from the menu.
3. Select the App grid from the bottom menu.

4. Set the size of the grid.
5. Select the Done option.

Apply A New Wallpaper Each Day

1. Touch and hold a blank area on your phone's Home screen.
2. Select the wallpaper and a theme from the menu.
3. Select the Wallpaper menu.
   - You can't use Daily wallpaper with custom wallpapers or live wallpapers.
4. Pick a genre of wallpapers to use.
5. In the upper-right corner, choose Daily wallpaper.
6. Tap Ok.

Include Icon Sets

To adjust icon colors to fit your phone's theme:

1. Touch and hold a blank area on your phone's Home screen.
2. Select the wallpaper and a theme from the menu.
3. Select Themed icons from the bottom menu to activate or deactivate.

Chapter Two
Customize Your Home Screens

Customize your Home screens by adding applications, shortcuts, and widgets.

You may arrange your Home screens in whatever way you choose for easy access to your preferred media. You may arrange and add:

- Apps
- In-app navigational shortcuts
- Non-app-launching information widgets

Some of these instructions only apply to Android 9 and later.

Insert Into Home Menus
You may add an app by

1. Swipe up from the bottom of the screen to access the Home screen.
2. Slide the app with your finger. There are pictures of all of the Home screens.
3. You may reposition the app by dragging it. Do the finger lifts.

Create a short clip

1. Touch the app, keep your finger there for a moment, and then release it. If the program supports shortcuts, a list will be shown.
2. To use, tap and hold the button.
3. Position the quick key by dragging it. Do the finger lifts.

A shortcut may be used even if it hasn't been saved to your Home screen by tapping on it.

Create a new widget or adjust the size of an existing one.

Put In A Gadget
1. Touch and hold an empty area on a Home screen.
2. Choose Extensions.
3. Tap and hold a piece of software. You will get screenshots of your Start menu.

4. Position the widget as you want it by dragging it. Do the finger lifts.

Widgets are a feature of several applications. To use, touch and hold the app. Select Widgets next.

Adjust The Size Of A Widget
1. Select the widget by touching and holding it on the Home screen.
2. Do the finger lifts. The outline of the widget will have dots on the sides if it can be enlarged.
3. Use the handles to resize the widget.
4. To dismiss the widget, touch it anywhere else on the screen.

Set Up Menus And Submenus
Create a new file (or group).

1. Just tap and hold the icon you want to use.
2. You may stack this app or shortcut by dragging it on top. Do the finger lift.
   - Adding additional requires a simple drag-and-drop action.
   - Simply touch the group to give it a name. Then, choose the recommended file naming convention. Choose from the list of recommended names located above the keyboard, or enter your own.

Changing the location of a program, widget, or group

1. Make use of your finger and pull the object around the screen. You will get screenshots of your Start menu.
2. The object may be slid to the desired location.
3. Do the finger lifts.

The "At a Glance" data at the top of your Pixel phone's screen is not movable.

Get rid of a program, button, or panel
1. Reach out and grab it.
2. Pull it up to the Remove menu.
3. Do the finger lifts.

You may encounter the words "Remove" and "Uninstall" or both. The "Remove" button merely deletes an app from the Home screen. Use the "Uninstall" button to permanently remove it from your mobile device.

The "At A Glance" data at the top of your Pixel phone's screen is not movable.

Arrange Start Menu Icons
Create a Start menu

1. Put your finger down and hold on an icon, menu, or folder.
2. To access a blank Home screen, slide it to the right.
3. Do the fingers lift.

Take away a Start menu

1. Take everything from the Home screens, including applications, shortcuts, widgets, and folders.
2. Once all of them are gone, there won't be a Home screen anymore.

Alter The Look Of the Start Menu
Modify heading information

The "At A Glance" data may be seen at the very top of the primary Home screen. You may discover details, for instance, on:

- Date
- Weather every day
- When do you have some free time?
- Notifications of parcel arrival from Nest
- Locating Your Bags After a Flight

If you want to modify the visible data:

1. Try holding your finger there.
2. Select Preferences / Modify / Settings.

Swap out a program

You may access a row of frequently used programs from the bottom of your screen.

- Deleting a well-liked program: To uninstall an app from your favorites, tap and hold it. Move it to a different screen location by dragging.
- Upload your most-used program: Swipe up from the bottom of the screen. To use, press and hold an app. insert the program into a free slot with your other favorites.

Modify Alternative Settings on the Home Screen

1. Touch and hold an empty area on the Home screen.
2. Make a selection under the "Household" options.

Adjust the animated status of the search bar.

In the Home screens search box, you may sometimes see animations. These animations are meant to be used just for festive occasions.

1. Touch and holding the search bar will disable or enable the animations.
2. Select Preferences by selecting more.
3. You can toggle the effects of the search box.

Swap Out Current Applications

The applications you use most often are lined up at the screen's bottom. Based on your latest and often-used applications and routines, your phone will provide suggestions for your favorites. The icons of the recommended programs you've selected all have colorful drop shadows.

A fresh app recommendation will be shown whenever there is a free slot in the row. Any of the recommended applications may be bookmarked, deleted, or added as needed. You may also replace any app with a manual change.

Stash away a program

1. To use the recommended app, press and hold it.
2. Select Pin from the menu's top right corner.

Take away a must-have program

1. To use the recommended app, press and hold it.
2. Select Pin from the menu's top right corner.

Touch and hold the app you want to prevent from being suggested, and then drop it on "Don't suggest app."

To disable recommended app updates for your preferred apps,

Recommendations will cease to appear until the function is activated again.

1. Touch and hold a blank area on your phone's Home screen.
2. Select Suggestions from the Home menu's settings.
3. You may toggle on/off:
   - Predictions in every app display Home screen Suggestions
   - Upload your preferred program

If you have disabled app recommendations in the Home screen settings, you will not be able to manually add a favorite app.

1. Swipe up from the bottom of the screen.
2. To use, press and hold an app.
3. Put the program where there is no other software currently installed.
4. Do the finger lifts.

Take Charge Of The Display

Take charge of the Pixel's display by adjusting its settings.

The options menu allows you to modify the screen's luminance, text size, display size, and rotation, among other things.

- You'll need Android 10 or later to complete some of these procedures.
- You'll need to use your fingers to go through some of these menus.

Adjust Your Screen's Resolution

1. Launch the device's configuration menu.
2. Click the screen.

3. Select the preference by tapping on it. Select "Advanced" to access further configuration options.

Use Quick Settings to quickly access your most often-used preferences from any interface.

Change Your Screen's Settings

Adjusting The Light Levels

- Light intensity

    Slide the Brightness level button to the desired brightness level.

- Light intensity regulation

    If you choose Adaptive brightness, your screen's brightness will automatically adjust to match the ambient light. By default, this setting will be active. While adaptive brightness is enabled, brightness adjustments are still possible. Your phone will gradually understand how you like to use it.

    In exceptionally strong ambient lighting, such as direct sunshine, adaptive brightness on the Pixel 4 and subsequent Pixel phones may momentarily brighten your screen over the typical maximum to make reading easier.

- Serious tone

    Select the gloomy background. Battery life may be extended by making the backdrop of certain phone displays darker. You may schedule certain times for the Dark theme to activate.

- Flashlight for the Night

    There are ways to improve your phone's usability when the lighting is poor.

Display Preferences

- Styles and wallpapers for desktop backgrounds (Pixel 2 and later): Modify the background, icon form, and color to make your phone uniquely yours.

- Background (just for Pixel 1): You may customize your background with a picture, a live wallpaper, or the default one.
- Related images

    You may customize the icon colors of compatible apps to fit the look of your phone.

- Serious tone

    Battery life may be extended by switching to a dark theme in some apps, such as the Settings menu. Select the gloomy background.

- Pause the screen

    You may adjust how long your phone's screen stays off between uses.

- Focus on the screen (Pixel 4 and later).

    Don't forget to leave your screen on while you're using it.

- Ambient EQ (Pixel 4 only) automatically adjusts your screen's color temperature to the light around you, which is especially helpful for screen attention when the screen is well-lit but not in direct sunlight.
- Effortless Screen (only on Pixel 4)

    Elevate the standard of most applications' scrolling and animations.

    While your phone is charging, you may see a screen saver that displays photographs, beautiful backdrops, and more.

- Hide the screen from the view
- Protect the screen: You may customize the way alerts appear behind the lock screen.
- Screen lock message put a custom message on your lock screen.
- Display lockdown choice.
- Time shown on two parallel lines: You may customize the lock screen clock to show either two or one line of time.
- Now Playing: Identify any music playing nearby in a flash.

- The screen turns on when you're close (only on Pixel 4) or stays on even when inactive.
- Don't hide the clock and other details (for all Pixel phones except the Pixel 4): You can still see the time and other information even if your screen is turned off.
- Click to check your phone: You may access hidden data by double-tapping the screen.
- In the lift, check the phone when you pick up your phone, look at the notifications.
- Updated alerts: Verify the lock screen for any new alerts.
- Colors
- Authentic: Your color perception will be spot on.
- Improved color accuracy and saturation. For Pixel 2, this is turned on automatically.
- See the most vibrant colors and retain color details with adaptive (Pixel 3 and later) technology. By default, this is enabled.
- Saturated mode (exclusive to Pixel 2) enhances color saturation.

Accessibility Options

- Text size

    Make text bigger or smaller on the screen.

- Dimensions shown

    Adjust the size of the text and other elements on the screen.

- Flip screen automatically

    The content on your screen will rotate as you spin your phone.

    You can still turn your screen by hand even if Auto-rotate is off. Turn your phone sideways and then hit the rotate button.

- Assuming the phone is in VR mode

    You may adjust your phone's VR settings to minimize blur or flicker.

Contact Emergency Services
Use your Google Pixel to contact emergency services.

To save and share your emergency contact information, download the Personal Safety app. Depending on where you are and whose service provider you use, your phone may automatically contact local emergency services.

You will need Android version 13 or later to complete any of these processes.

Get Ready For A Crisis

Lock screen messages and emergency contact information are always visible to anybody who picks up your phone, so don't bother locking it. The Personal Safety app allows you to disable this feature.

Use the App for Your Safety

Every Pixel has the option to download the free Personal Safety app. All Pixel 4 and later devices will automatically get the app.

Disabling the Personal Safety app will not delete it from your device.

Install The Emergency Assistance App
Install the Emergency Assistance app on a Pixel 3a or before.

1. Verify that you're running the most recent version of Android.
2. The About section may be accessed by selecting Settings.
3. Select the Emergency menu.
4. The update may be accessed by tapping the banner at the top of the screen.

If you don't see the banner, you may already have the Personal Safety app installed. Make sure you're using the most recent version available on the Play Store.

Possible Actions

- If you have a Pixel 3a or an older model, even if you haven't installed the app: Sign in with your Google Account to add medical information and emergency contacts.
- When downloading the app: Emergency SOS, Emergency Sharing, Safety Checks, Crisis Alerts, and Car Crash Detection are all available to you. Only devices starting with the Pixel 3 are capable of auto crash detection.

Needed Items

Turn on Location Services and provide the Personal Safety app access to your location. There are restrictions on which countries and which categories of users may participate in Location Sharing.

With the help of Location Sharing, you may let people know exactly where you are at any given moment. Your friend or family member may see your name, picture, and current position across all Google services, including Google Maps when you share your location with them. The details of your shared location could include:

- Where you are right now or where you've been.
- What you're doing right now, whether it walking or driving.
- Information unique to your device, such as battery life or GPS availability.
- Whether you've just "started a call" or "called the local emergency number."
- Locations such as where you live, work, and travel.

Including crucial information in the Personal Safety app

Your blood type, allergies, and prescribed medicines may all be stored in your phone's secure area.

1. Launch the phone's security app.
2. Log in with your Google Account if prompted.
3. Check out the data.
4. Put in your own contact and medical information in case of an emergency.
   - Regarding Health-Related Data:
   - Listen to Health records.

- You may edit information like allergies and medicines by tapping the item in the list.
- For Use in Case of an Emergency:
- The steps are as follows: choose Emergency contacts > Add contact > The name of the current contact you want to add.

Tips:

- When your screen is locked, you may still access your emergency contacts by tapping Allow access to emergency details and selecting Show when locked.
- Connect your phone to a SIM card or electronic SIM. Your phone won't be able to send a message to an emergency contact if you don't.

Start monitoring for car crashes

In the event of a major automobile accident, your phone may instantly contact emergency services (such as 911 in the United States) and relay your position.

- Car collision detection requires a SIM card in your phone.
- Car collision detection is supported in the following languages on Pixel 3 and subsequent devices: languages spoken in Denmark, the Netherlands, England, France, France (Canada), Italy, Japan, China (Mandarin), Norway, Spain, and Sweden. For the Americas, Australia, Canada, Europe, Asia, Oceania, Oceania, Europe, Far East, France, Ireland, Italy, Japan, Norway, the Netherlands, Singapore, Spain, Sweden, Taiwan, the United Kingdom, and the United States.
1. Launch the phone's security app.
2. Select Options.
3. Look for the section under "Car Crash Detection."
4. Choose Options.
   - When prompted to disclose your location when using the app, choose Allow.
   - Allow access to your microphone and location when prompted.

Auto Crash Detection
The Science behind Auto Crash Detection

- Pixel 3, 4, and later phones may analyze data including your location, motion sensors, and surrounding noises to predict a probable serious automobile collision. Location, motion, and access to a microphone are all needed for collision detection in automobiles. Your phone can automatically contact emergency services if it detects an automobile accident. Android's Emergency Calling feature may communicate your current location and incident details.
- Not all collisions will be detected by your phone. Emergency services may be called in response to high-impact events. It's possible that your Pixel phone won't be able to contact 911 in an emergency. It's possible, for instance, that your phone is now engaged in a call or linked to a slow mobile network.

Make a selection to activate or deactivate the emergency signal

Use your phone's emergency features, such as phoning for assistance, notifying others of your location, and capturing video, to get you through a sticky situation.

- Car collision detection requires a SIM card in your phone. Discover SIM card installation.
- When Battery Saver or Airplane Mode is on, Emergency SOS will not send out a signal.
- Pixels starting with the 3 have access to Emergency SOS.

Put Out An SOS Signal
1. Launch the phone's Security & Emergency app.
2. Select Options.
3. Click the button labeled "Emergency SOS."
4. Choose Options.
5. When an emergency occurs, you may set Emergency SOS to perform a predetermined set of actions. Activate the features you intend to use:
   - Dial 9-1-1 immediately: When an emergency arises, call the appropriate number in your area. If your area has many emergency contact options, dial 911 first. Select the Number to call to swap the outgoing caller ID. Once you've settled on a new figure, hit "Save."

- Inform those who can help in an emergency: Send your current location and any changes to your emergency contacts in real-time.
- Document critical situations by recording: Take a video and save/back it up/share it with your emergency contacts.
- Dissemination on autopilot: Once you've completed a backup, you may instantly send a download link to anybody you've designated as an emergency contact. When you are through recording, you will have the option to stop sharing.

Disable The Panic Button
1. Launch the phone's Security & Emergency app.
2. Select Options.
3. Disable the SOS emergency function.

Make your lock screen say anything

1. Start the phone's configuration program.
2. Toggle the screen and Screen lock This was followed by the Put a note on the locked screen.
3. Put in your message, such as contact information in case someone finds your missing phone.
4. Pick the Save option.

Manage Mass Notifications in Case of Emergencies

This option allows you to choose how you get critical communications like AMBER alerts, threat notifications, and other similar alerts.

Sound and vibration may be adjusted, and you can enable or disable different sorts of notifications.

1. Launch the phone's Settings menu.
2. Select Alerts, followed by Wireless Emergency Alerts.
3. Decide how frequently you want to be notified and what options you want to activate.

Call For Assistance
In an emergency, call for assistance.

Seek medical attention after a vehicle collision (Pixel 3+ only)

Using Battery Saver or Airplane mode will disable crash detection while driving. Mobile phone crash alerts only function in the nation associated with the SIM card in your phone.

If you have already activated automobile accident detection on your phone and it detects a major automobile collision:

1. The phone will buzz, ring, and display an on-screen and audible prompt asking whether you need assistance.
2. React in under a minute:
    - In case of an emergency, dial: You may either use the word "Emergency" or hit the emergency button twice. The phone will switch to speaker mode without your intervention.
    - How to End a Call Click "Cancel" or "I'm Good" to cancel. A 911 call won't be placed from your phone.
    - If no reply: When an automobile accident is detected, your phone will immediately dial 911, go into speaker mode, report the incident, and provide its location.

    You may interrupt the repeating message by talking over it. Select Cancel to end the message but keep the call going.

Call for assistance, notify your connections, and film a video all using Emergency SOS.

Emergency SOS is disabled when using airplane mode or the Battery Saver setting.

Use your phone's emergency features, such as phoning for assistance, notifying others of your location, and capturing video, to get you through a sticky situation.

1. Press the power button on your phone at least five times.
2. There will be a 5-second countdown before immediate action is taken. During the countdown, you may cancel the emergency activities if you accidentally activated Emergency SOS.
3. You may configure what happens once the countdown ends (5 seconds). While making a call to emergency services, any emergency sharing or video recording you've enabled will begin automatically.

Take a video in case of an emergency

To better ensure your safety in the case of an emergency, it is highly recommended that you always have a video recording device on hand. We may keep track of your usage of the application, sharing with emergency contacts, and video link views/downloads when you use the capabilities of our products to record, upload, and/or share video and audio material, such as recordings of an emergency, in addition to the information we collect as described in our Privacy Policy. Your emergency contacts may be upset if you record the events of an emergency and send them to them. Be cautious while uploading and sharing videos. When utilizing this function, you are responsible for adhering to any local, state, and federal laws, such as those about video recording and wiretapping. You agree to the above by making use of this function.

Mechanisms Of Emergency Audio Recording
With emergency recording enabled, you may still use your phone to call emergency services and share your location with loved ones.

The emergency recording will stop if you switch to another app that requires the usage of your camera. Your recording will go to a gray screen when emergency recording is halted. You may access your recorded message in an emergency by either reopening the Personal Safety app or by tapping the notification bar at the top of your screen.

The maximum recording time for emergency recording is 45 minutes. About 10 megabytes per minute might be expected from the video's quality.

Exactly How Automatic Sharing Works
Once you've recorded a video, if you enable auto share, a link to it will be sent to anybody you've designated to get emergency notifications. No one will see your video unless you've set up Emergency Contacts. You have 15 seconds after the recording begins to change your mind about sharing the video. The time it takes to upload and share your video after you've finished filming may vary depending on the speed of your internet connection. A copy of your video may be downloaded by anybody you've designated as an emergency contact.

At any one moment, only one of a video's share links will be active. The links you generate will automatically expire after 7 days for your security. At any moment, you may disable a link. Remove the current link's activation and create a new one to reset the timer. Disabling a share button entails:

1. Launch the phone's Security & Emergency app.
2. Select "Your Information" and "Your Videos."
3. Select More, then Delete, and finally Delete next to the video you want to remove.

This emergency recording is for your use only in the event of an actual emergency. If a link is being shared too often, Google will deactivate it automatically. More than 120 clicks on the shareable link constitute excessive sharing.

The inner workings of an automatic backup system

During an emergency, all recordings made will be transferred to the cloud immediately. If your phone is ever lost or damaged, this will help keep your information safe. If you're using a metered connection, uploading to the cloud might end up costing you money. Anytime and wherever with an internet connection, you may access the uploaded emergency recordings. Video organization involves:

1. Launch the phone's Security & Emergency app.
2. Select "Your Information" and "Your Videos."
3. To delete or share a video, hit more on the button next to it.

A file that is deleted from your Google Account cannot be recovered under any circumstances.

Obtain crucial safety data

1. If your device is locked, swipe up.
2. Dial 9-1-1, and then Check out the urgent information.

Automatically transmit your current location

When you call 911 in the United States or 112 in Europe, your phone will automatically provide your position to emergency personnel.

If you haven't disabled Android's Emergency Location Service (ELS), your phone will automatically broadcast its location to emergency personnel if and only if ELS is enabled in your nation or area and on your mobile network. Even if you have turned off ELS, your cell provider may still share your location if you make an emergency call or send a text.

Modify The Emergency Location Service
Modify the status of the Emergency Location Service.

1. Launch the phone's Settings menu.
2. The Emergency Location Service and Google Emergency Location Service will appear under Location once you choose Location and then Location services.
3. Adjust the status of the Emergency Location Service or the Google Emergency Location Service.

The Operation of the Emergency Locator Service

Only while making an emergency call or sending a text message will your phone activate its Emergency Location Service (ELS).

When an emergency call is made from a phone with ELS enabled, ELS may utilize data from Google position Services and other sources to pinpoint the user's exact position. Additional data, such as the language settings for your device, may be sent over ELS as well.

If you have permitted emergency response agencies to access your location and contact information, your phone will do so. Your phone's GPS coordinates are sent straight to emergency responders without going via Google.

When you hang up an ELS-enabled call or text, your phone will submit information to Google about your use, statistics, and diagnostics via Google Play Services. Without receiving any personally identifiable information, including your location, Google can assess how effectively ELS works.

Sending your location with ELS works differently than sharing it with a service like Google Maps.

Tell others where you are in case of an emergency.

Your emergency contacts may track your whereabouts in real-time and get regular updates on your battery status. For the Personal Safety app to work, you'll need to allow it to access your location.

A notification will show up in the Personal Safety app if Location Sharing is off in your country.

Sharing in an emergency requires:

- Establish at least one point of contact in case of an unexpected event.
- To use the Personal Safety app, location access "While in Use" must be granted.
- Turn on Location Services and ensure you can access the internet.

Initiate Immediate Mutual Aid

1. Launch the phone's security app.
2. Select the "Emergency" option.
3. You may pick and choose who can see your current location.
    - A custom message is available.
4. Invoke the Share button.
5. You may check out what information you shared in an emergency by tapping the banner notice.

Put an end to Extinction Rallying

1. Launch the phone's security app.
2. Use the data-sharing system in case of an emergency.
3. Reduce taps to stop.
    - You may provide the reason for canceling the emergency contribution.

After 24 hours, emergency sharing will automatically stop.

Plan a safety inspection.

Schedule a safety check to have your phone check in on you and alert your designated emergency contacts if anything seems amiss.

You may do a safety check whether going to a party or exploring a new place. Using the Personal Safety app requires you to provide "While in Use" access to your device's location.

1. Launch the phone's Security & Emergency app.
2. It's time to double-check the tap's safety.
3. Choose a Justification and Timeframe. The time range for the check is between 15 minutes and 8 hours in the future.
4. Then proceed by selecting Next.
5. Pick out some buddies.
6. Select the "Start" button.

During an emergency, your contacts will get a text message containing:

- I'm calling you by your name.
- How long your security measure will last.
- If you gave me a reason, which I doubt.

Put A Check Besides Your Name
You'll receive a warning 60 seconds before Emergency sharing starts to let you know it's time to check-in. If you verify that you are okay, we will stop the Emergency sharing. At any moment, you may dismiss the Safety check alert. Failure to respond within 60 seconds will trigger Emergency sharing.

1. Select an option when you receive the alert:
   - I'm OK. Avoid Sharing.
   - Let the sharing begin! With this, we will no longer conduct safety inspections.
   - Call 911.
2. Your phone may need unlocking if it is now inaccessible.

Even if your phone dies or loses service, Safety checks will continue to function. At the predetermined check-in time, Emergency contact information will be shared based on your last known location.

How to Contact People in Case of an Emergency

As soon as you activate Emergency sharing, Google will send a message to your emergency contacts that include:

- It's your name
- A connection to your current location as shown on Google Maps.
- How much battery life you have left
- Any message you want to leave

Marking yourself as safe or turning off Emergency sharing is an option. After Google's safety checks are complete, another SMS is sent to your contacts.

Learn of Emergencies

When you enable Crisis alerts in the Personal Safety app, you'll get notifications in the event of a national or regional emergency, such as a natural catastrophe. When a crisis occurs, the Personal Safety app will send you a notice and a link to its webpage so you may learn more.

All nations and languages may get the notifications. The notice may appear in the official language of the country in which you are now located if your phone is set to a language other than the local language.

Adjust Your Crisis Alert Settings
1. Launch the phone's security app.
2. Select Crisis notifications from the Features menu.
3. Set your preference for receiving crisis warnings.

Details about Google's emergency notification system

Google coordinates data collection from local authorities during times of crisis. The Personal Safety app will alert you whenever a crisis is reported that is relevant to your locality. Google issues crisis warnings depending on criteria such as internet access in the region, official information from governments and other agencies, and the effect on the ground. Usually, both the local languages and English are included in alerts.

When an emergency arises, quickly dial 911.

Even if you have locked your phone, you can still swiftly contact 911.

Create a phone number that may be used in case of an emergency.

The Personal Safety app lets you choose many ways to get in touch with 911:

- The Fast Emergency Dialer (FED) is a slider-based emergency calling system. Automatically shown are the local emergency numbers.
- The traditional emergency dialer (TED) displays a telephone keypad that may be used to contact 911.

Pixel phones are preconfigured to automatically use FED in areas where it is offered.

Quick SOS Calling Capabilities

- Easy access to Make a speedy phone call using the slider to choose an emergency contact.
- Automatically dialed 911: Even when you're abroad, your phone will instantly locate emergency services.
- Alternatives to 911: Your phone automatically searches for local emergency services including police, fire, and medical help. Select the appropriate ambulance service using the slider.

Quickly Calling an Emergency Number
Android 11 and earlier, including Android 12 on the Pixel 5 and before, provide a shortcut for turning the device on and off:

1. Put in a five-second hold on the power button.
2. In Case of an Emergency, Dial *.
3. Use the slider in the quick menu if you need help.

On Android 12 and the Pixel 6 and later, the power and volume buttons do the following by default:

1. To increase the volume, simultaneously press the Power button and the up arrow button.
2. In Case of an Emergency, Dial *.
3. Use the slider in the quick menu if you need help.

Access To An Emergency Calling Service

Not all locations or regions provide FED service. Even if you live in a covered region, your carrier and other factors may restrict your access to FED.

If FED is unavailable, your phone will switch over to TED, which will provide you with a dial pad from which you may make 911 calls. Yours presets for the emergency phone don't update when FED isn't working.

Use The Help Of An Operator

When an emergency number (such as 911 in the United States) is dialed on a Pixel phone, the "Emergency Number" screen appears.

- The majority of 911 operators should be familiar with these options (you can always make a regular phone call).
- You don't even need a working computer!
- Nothing to set up

Determine where you are in a crisis

The emergency operator will be able to read your position from your screen. Depending on the capabilities of your phone, you may discover:

- Exact postal address
- Added symbols (such as "CWC8+JH")
- Longitude and latitude may be expressed simply using plus codes.
- Responders in emergencies will identify them.
- Geographic coordinates (such as "37.4216105,-122.0857449")
- Map

Send a quiet signal to a nearby operator (in certain areas).

Only users in Australia, France, Italy, Taiwan, the United Kingdom, and the United States may access this function.

Tap the Medical, Fire, or Police button to contact an operator without having to speak.

Nothing will happen to your phone. However, here's what the 911 operator will hear:

- That it is a voice-activated computer system
- The kind of assistance you need
- Where you are from (only in the US, UK, and Australia)
- Name (if known through Emergency Contacts or other device settings)

Locate Earthquake Information

When an earthquake occurs nearby, your phone will alert you. Start by typing "earthquake in [your city or region]" into Google Search to get details on recent tremors in your area.

Disable Google Location Accuracy to prevent your phone from aiding in earthquake detection.

Sign Up For Earthquake Warnings
Sign up for earthquake warnings in your area

State of California, State of Oregon State of Washington

Your phone can notify you about nearby earthquakes of magnitude 4.5 or higher based on your approximate location. The information for these earthquake warnings comes from the website ShakeAlert.

Grecians and Kiwis

Your phone can notify you about nearby earthquakes of magnitude 4.5 or higher based on your approximate location. These notifications are derived from Android's Earthquake Alerts System.

Adjust your quake notifications on and off.

You must have your wireless connection or mobile data switched on for notifications to work.

1. Launch the device's configuration menu.
2. A/V Emergency & Safety and then there were seismic warnings.
3. Change your settings for quake notifications.

The setting for earthquake warnings is always on. Not every earthquake in your region will trigger an alert, and notifications will only be sent to users in countries where the service is actively maintained. On rare occasions, you may get a warning for an earthquake but not feel it where you are.

Chapter Three
Use Your Pixel To Go About

Use your Pixel phone as a navigation device

Some of these instructions need Android 11 or later. Find out how to verify your Android version.

Pick A Mode Of Transportation

1. Start the phone's configuration program.
2. Select Gestures, then System, and finally System settings.
3. Just choose one:
   - Hand gestures are used instead of buttons.
   - There are three buttons for use in navigating the app: "Home," "Back," and "Overview."
   - With the Pixel 3, 3 XL, 3a, and 3a XL, you can navigate with just two buttons—Home and Back.

Switch Between Windows
Switch between windows, websites, and programs

Turn around

Bring up the previous window you were using. Multiple visits are permitted. The Home screen is the last screen you may return to.

- To move around the screen using a gesture, swipe from the left or right side.
- There are three buttons you may use to go where you need to go.
- Tap Back for 2-button navigation on Pixel 3, 3 XL, 3a, and 3a XL.

Access the Main Menu

- Using just your finger, swipe up from the bottom of the screen to navigate.
- You may use the standard Home button or the back and menu buttons.
- Pixel 3, Pixel 3 XL, Pixel 3a, and Pixel 3a XL only have a Home button.

You can set up several Home screens. To switch between them, just swipe right or left.

Determine all currently active software

- Move around using a swipe up from the bottom, a brief pause, and a release.
- Using the standard "Overview" button (one of three) will take you to the main menu.
- For Pixel 3, 3 XL, 3a, and 3a XL, the two-button navigation is a swipe from the bottom of the screen to the center.

It is possible to:

- Exit programs: Lift the app icon with a swipe.
- Start a program: Pick its representation by tapping on it.
- Get a screenshot of that: Select Screenshot from the menu.
- Pick a language and then pick some text: Select may be tapped. You may then use the app's picture to pick words to copy, share, or search.

You can't choose text from all applications or capture a screenshot using 2-button navigation.

Change between programs

- To use the gesture controls, swipe from left to right at the very bottom of the screen.
- Using the standard "Overview" button (one of three) will take you to the main menu. To access the desired app, just swipe right. Tap it.
- If you're using a Pixel 3a or an older model, you can access your two most recently used applications by swiping right on Home.

Reach your various app menus

- To use gesture controls, swipe up from the bottom or the center of the screen.
- To access the three buttons, swipe up from the bottom or the center of the screen.

- To access the two buttons, swipe up from the center of the home screen.

Google your phone (starting with Pixel 4)

When you use the search on your Pixel phone, it will look for results both locally and online.

- Internet: Search Engine Results
- Apps: App-based software and content
- Relationships: the people in your life and the software you use to keep in touch with them
- Adjustments: Personalization of your phone's software and data settings
- Shop on Google's Play: Android Market Applications
- Screenshots: Miniature versions of current mobile screen captures
- Actions in the Google Assistant app that may be used to do tasks including scheduling, messaging, and more
- Advice for Your Pixel: Pixel-only cheats, features, and updates
  1. To use the search function on your mobile device, just press or slide up on the home screen.
  2. Simply enter your search terms into the box provided, choose the result you want to see in full by tapping on it or continue scrolling to view further results.

Shift Things Around

Check off or shift things

Select with a tap

You may pick or launch an app by tapping its icon. Some applications let you do activities such as booking a reservation or playing music by touching and holding text.

Swipe to edit

Tap the space where you want to start typing. A keyboard will be ready for use.

Physical contact and holding

Select an option and hold your finger there. Once the object has responded, take your finger off it.

Drag

Tap and hold to move something. Simply move your finger across the screen without lifting it. Raise your index finger when it rests on the correct spot. One feature is the ability to drag and drop applications anywhere on the Home screen.

Drag or flick

Swipe your finger quickly and continuously over the screen. Swiping left or right on a Home screen, for instance, can provide other Home screen options.

Modify the proportions and placement of things.

Double-tap to zoom in/out

You may "zoom in" (get a closer look) by tapping a page twice.

To enlarge or reduce, pinch and spread.

Some applications allow you to adjust the font size by tapping the screen with two or more fingers. Reduce your size by squeezing your fingers together. To expand, separate them.

Rotate

Most smartphone displays can spin in tandem with the user's palm. Swipe down with two fingers from the top and touch Auto-rotate to enable or disable rotation.

Easily Adjust Your Pixel's Settings

Quick Settings makes it possible to access and modify system preferences without having to go through many menus. You may customize your experience by putting frequently adjusted parameters in a "Quick Settings" panel.

Some of these instructions need Android 11 or later.

Invoke Fast Preferences

1. Swipe down from the top of the screen to see the primary configuration options.
2. Swipe down once more to access the Quick Settings menu.

Adjustable On/Off Switches

- Just touch the switch to activate or deactivate it. The lights have not been dimmed.
- The longer you touch and hold a setting, the more possibilities you'll see.

Change, Delete, Or Reposition

1. Swipe down twice from the screen's top.
2. Select Edit in the leftmost menu.
3. Make sure to touch and hold the setting for it to take effect.
4. Move the slider to the desired position.
    - Hold and drag to add tiles, and then rise to add a new option.
    - Simply drop the unwanted option where it says "Drag here to remove."

Adjust The Volume And Video

The media player allows you to stop, rewind, and adjust playback parameters. Swipe down from the top of your screen to see what's now playing on your phone.

Tip:

- Inquiries to include an app's tile in the Quick Settings menu are made by a subset of applications. These may be turned off or on whenever you choose.
- Sometimes, phones may conceal icons to free up screen real estate if you have a lot of options activated at once. A dot at the top of your phone's screen will lead you to the hidden icons.

Manage The Sound And Video

- Swipe down from the top of your screen to see what's now playing on your phone.
- Tap the panel to launch the media player app.
- Swipe to the right or left to switch between your various media apps.

- Tap the name of your audio attachment in the upper right panel to alter where the sound plays. Some examples of these include "speakers" and "pixel buds."

File Searching And Deletion
Google Pixel phone file searching and deletion

The Files app on your Pixel phone is often the place to look for downloaded files.

- You'll need Android 10 or later to complete some of these procedures.
- You'll need to use touch input for a few of these tasks.

File Browsing And Opening
1. The Files app must be launched.
2. The data you've downloaded will appear.
   - Select Menu to browse for further data.
   - Select More, then Sort by, and then enter a name, date, type, or size to arrange the list.
3. Tap the file you want to open.

Clear Up Your Pixel's Storage
1. The Files app must be launched.
2. Select a file with a tap.
3. Select Delete, followed by Delete.

Distribute, Print, And Save
You can do things like distribute, print, and save on Google Drive.

The Pixel phone has built-in file sharing.

1. Use your hands to grip the file.
2. Select the Share button.

You may also take extra steps, such as printing or saving to Google Drive.

1. Tap the file you want to open.

2. Look for more controls in the upper right corner. For more, click here.

Discover New Media To Like

Several applications allow users to download media content, such as movies or novels. If you're looking for the app you got it from, that's where you'll find it.

Put Data On A Computer

When your phone is connected to a computer through USB, the files on your phone will show up in the "Downloads" folder on your PC.

Use Digital Wellbeing To Regulate

Pixel users may use Digital Wellbeing to regulate their smartphone use.

You can find out details on your phone usage, like as how frequently you unlock it and how long you spend in each app, using a Pixel phone. That knowledge will help you take better care of your digital health. App timers and scheduled display updates are only two examples.

- You'll need Android 10 or later to complete some of these procedures.
- You'll need to use touch input for a few of these tasks.

Initiate Online Health Monitoring

Launch the Settings menu and toggle the toggle next to the Digital Wellbeing entry to make the app's symbol visible in the app drawer.

Digital Wellbeing requires you to create a profile the first time you use it.

1. Launch the device's configuration menu.
2. Look at Digital Health and safety settings for kids.
3. Select the option to Display Data under "Your Digital Wellbeing Resources."

If you have the default parent account on a child's device, you can also manage their account.

App-Based Time Management

Consider your app use habits.

1. Start the phone's configuration program.
2. Look at Digital Health and safety settings for kids.
3. Today's phone activity is shown graphically. Hit the graph for details. For instance:
   - How long and which applications you've been using might be categorized as "screen time."
   - The frequency with which you unlock your phone and access certain applications.
   - How many and from what applications you've received alerts
4. Tap an icon to access the app's settings or learn more about it.

You should regulate the amount of time you spend using apps daily.

Not all workplaces or educational institutions support app-based timers.

1. Start the phone's configuration program.
2. Look at Digital Health and safety settings for kids.
3. Select an item on the graph with a tap.
4. Select the program you'd want to restrict and then select Set Timer.
5. Set a time limit for how long you may stay on the app. Then choose "Set."

When your time is over, the app will shut and its symbol will fade. Remember that app timers often start again at midnight.

- If you want to use the app again before midnight, just erase the app timer using steps 1-4 above.
- Time management with Google Chrome

Determine Your Days

Determine how much of your day is spent perusing the web.

1. Launch the device's configuration utility.
2. Look at Digital Health and safety settings for kids.
3. Toggle the graph This was followed by the All chromed out.

- If you can't locate it immediately, try selecting Show all applications.
4. Drag and drop Display the URLs you go to, and choose Display. You can see which sites you visited and for how long daily.
5. Tap the site's name to get your visit duration details.

Subvert Previous Site Visits
Simply tapping a webpage on the history list will disable its display. Select Remove visits from the past and then remove them at the bottom. It will be on the list again if you revisit the site in the future.

Daily Internet time limits should be set.

1. Launch the device's configuration utility.
2. Look at Digital Health and safety settings for kids.
3. Toggle the graph after that, and a blank screen.
   - If you can't locate it immediately, try selecting Show all applications.
4. Select Set site timer next to the URL you'd want to time out.
5. Set a timer and then press the OK button.

Bed Down With Nighttime Mode
Verify snoring and coughing records.

The Digital Wellbeing app is not designed to replace professional medical advice. The goal is to provide you with the knowledge that will allow you to strike a comfortable technological equilibrium. Please see a physician if you have any health concerns. Google makes no claims about the functionality or consequences of this product.

This function may only be accessed with the most recent version of the Digital Wellbeing app.

The clock on your phone to verify the information.

1. Launch the Clock app on your device.
2. Listen to the Sleep Machine.
   - Under "Show cough and snore activity," choose to Continue and then Allow if this is your first time using Bedtime mode.

You may choose between the Bedtime activity and the Cough and Snore activity by tapping the Bedtime button.

Verify your Digital well-being stats now.

1. Launch the phone's Settings menu.
2. Try out the Family Settings and Digital Well-Being options.
3. For the option to "Show cough & snore activity," choose Continue.

Your cough and snoring data will be saved in the "Bedtime mode" section of the Digital Wellbeing app.

Go on a data hunt

1. Launch the phone's Settings menu.
2. Select Search from the menu bar.
3. Put in the word "cough."
4. Select Cough & Snore to launch the Digital Wellbeing app.

How to Establish a Nightly Routine

1. Launch the phone's Settings menu.
2. Select "Digital Well-being & parental controls," "Bedtime mode," and "Bedtime routine" from the menu that appears.
3. Set the time when the bedtime feature will activate.
4. Establish a nighttime ritual through one of two means:
   - According to a timetable: Choose the days of the week on which you want to sleep and the hours between which you want to sleep.
   - Set an "After" and "Before" time and charge your phone between those two points each night.

Use the fast settings toggle to rapidly activate or deactivate the Bedtime mode.

Put all those applications on hold for a while

1. Start the phone's configuration program.
2. Focus mode may be accessed by selecting Digital Wellbeing & parental controls.

3. Pick and choose which programs to put on hold. You won't be able to use these applications or get alerts from them while Focus mode is active.
4. If you need to concentrate without interruptions, go to Focus mode.
   - Focus mode may be activated or deactivated by tapping the respective toggle at the top of the screen.
   - Select the Schedule button to have Focus mode activate at predetermined times.
   - When in Focus mode, tapping Take a Break and setting a timer will allow you to resume work on your applications.

Quick Settings on certain phones allow you to toggle on focus mode quickly.

Walk with as little interruption as possible (Pixel 2 and after).

When you activate Heads Up, you'll get encouraging prompts to take your eyes off your phone and back to the road.

To activate or deactivate Heads Up:

1. Start the phone's configuration program.
2. Heads Up may be accessed by selecting Digital Wellbeing & parental controls.
   - Simply comply with the on-screen prompts to set up Heads Up.
   - If you press the switch next to "Heads Up," it will disable the feature.

Minimize disruptions

The settings for your digital health will allow you to make any necessary adjustments. Find out how to:

- Control alerts
- Hand motions to turn off the phone
- Keep distractions to a minimum with the help of the Do Not Disturb button.

Use Automated Driving Mode
Put your Pixel phone into automated driving mode.

When you're driving, you may activate Do Not Disturb while also using Android Auto on a Pixel 3 or later. You may activate Do Not Disturb when driving with your Pixel 2.

If you want to use your phone while driving safely:

- You may turn off your phone completely by using the "Do Not Disturb" feature.
- Use Android Auto's driving mode if you need to use your phone while driving.
- Utilize the car's display instead of the car's driving mode to utilize Android Auto. Explore Android Auto's features.

Configure Driving Settings
Starting with Pixel 3: Configure driving settings

1. Start the phone's configuration program.
2. Select Drive Mode from Connected Devices > Connection Preferences > Drive Mode.
3. Behavior is a Tap.
   - Open Android Auto to use your phone hands-free while driving.
   - If you want to avoid using your phone while driving, choose Do Not Disturb from the menu.
4. Select the auto-start option.
   - Starting with Pixel 3: Select "When connected via Bluetooth" if you want to use your car's Bluetooth connection. Now choose your vehicle.
   - Only the Pixel 3: Select When driving is detected if your vehicle does not support Bluetooth.

The Pixel 3 and subsequent models can determine whether you have been in a vehicle accident.

Set A Traffic Regulation

1. Start the phone's configuration program.
2. Do not disturb, and then tap the sound.

3. Select the auto-start option.
4. Select "Add Rule" followed by "Driving."
5. Make sure your rule is active up top.

To get rid of the rule, use the Delete button.

Switch On/Off Driver Mode

When does your phone activate "driver mode"?

- An automobile can hook up to it.
- A moving automobile is what it imagines itself to be.

After approximately, the phone's driving mode will turn off.

- Walk for 30 seconds
- Inactivity for 10 minutes

Use For Contactless Payments

If a store accepts contactless payments, you may utilize the tap-and-pay method to make a purchase.

Some of these instructions need Android 11 or later.

Activate Near Field Communication

Your phone doesn't support NFC if you can't find the option to enable it there. No contactless payments will be accepted.

1. Start the phone's configuration program.
2. Select NFC from the Connected devices' Connection options.
3. Allow NFC access.

Control Contactless Payment Applications

1. Activate Contactless payments if you want to use them.
2. To make a Contactless payment, use the appropriate app.
3. Start the phone's configuration program.
4. Select NFC from the list of connected devices and then tap Connection options.
5. Select Payment default after tapping Contactless Payments.
6. Select a default app to use for making purchases.

The Settings option will only appear if the relevant payment app supports contactless transactions. Mobile payment systems are incompatible with money transfer applications. Apps for making purchases are readily available in the Google Play app store.

Access Your Cards And Passes
Push the button to access your cards and passes.

If you use the Google Pay app to make contactless payments, you may access your Google Pay payment methods and passes by pressing the power button. The Settings app also serves as a toggle for the card and passes functionality.

To access your cards and passes by pressing the power button, you must have Google Pay installed and set up.

1. Launch the device's configuration utility.
2. Card readers and gesture controls come after the tap system.
3. Control the use of cards and passes.

Blocking Of Contactless Payments
Repair the blocking of contactless payments caused by unauthorized card reading

If your battery dies rapidly and your phone's contactless payments app isn't functioning, you may be too near to a payment card or other object with an NFC chip. If you have any payment cards stored in a wallet-style phone case, try taking the case off and seeing if it helps.

Your phone's NFC sensor will keep trying to communicate with any nearby NFC chips, such as those found in payment cards and other items.

Even if another case seems to suit your phone, it is still recommended that you choose one made specifically for your phone's model.

A phone's NFC sensor's location may be found by studying a schematic of the device.

Stop All Contactless Transactions
Disabling NFC will also disable any other functionality that relies on it.

1. Start the phone's configuration program.
2. Select NFC from the list of connected devices and then tap Connection options.
3. Switch off NFC use.

You may disable contactless payments by opening your payment app. This feature isn't available in all mobile payment applications.

Locate Nearby Hardware
Locate nearby hardware and get it set up.

Using your Pixel phone, you may locate and activate nearby equipment.

- You'll need Android 10 or later to complete some of these procedures.
- You'll need to use touch input for a few of these tasks.

Install New Equipment
New equipment should be installed near you.

Phone Setup
1. Do this on your phone right now if you haven't already if you want to avoid missing out:
   - Get your Bluetooth on!
   - Get Location turned on.
2. If you have your device's alerts turned off, please enable them.

Installing The New Equipment
Fast Pair allows you to quickly and easily pair up compatible devices including Chromecast, Wear OS watches, other Android phones and tablets, and more. The packaging of quick pair compatible accessories will specify that fact. Most also have the phrase "Made by Google" or "Made for Google."

1. Start up a brand-new gadget that hasn't been configured yet. Place the gadget in its "pairing" mode.
2. Open the display on your mobile device.
3. You'll see a prompt on your phone to set up the new gadget.
4. Click on the alert.
5. Just stick to the on-screen prompts.

Modify The Alert Settings

Notifications of adjacent devices that you may configure will appear automatically. Even if you disable alerts, you may see nearby devices using your phone's Settings menu.

1. Start the phone's configuration program.
2. Select Devices & Sharing> Google > Devices.
3. You may toggle the option to scan for adjacent devices.

Repair Device Setup Issues

- Check your device's settings if you don't get a notice. Then, there's Google, followed by Devices & Sharing. This is followed by the section on gadgets.
- Make sure you're not too far away from the gadget. Fast Pair requires that your compatible accessories be within 0.5 m (1.6 ft) of your phone.
- Activate Bluetooth and your phone's location services.
- Make sure your mobile device can access the internet by checking its network settings.

Not all devices can be detected and set up automatically by your phone. If a gadget isn't showing up in your Settings app, you can always use Bluetooth to link up with it.

Utilize The Data Saver

Data Saver helps you save on mobile data use.

If you have a restricted mobile data plan, you may reduce your data use by using Data Saver. In this mode, Wi-Fi is the sole source of background data for most applications and services. Mobile data may be used by already running applications and services.

Android 8.0 or later is required for some of the instructions below.

Adjust The Data Saver Setting

1. Start the phone's configuration program.
2. Utilize the Web and Network Then there was Data Saver.
3. Flip the switch for Data Saver.
    - The Data Saver symbol will appear in your status bar whenever this feature is active.

- A notice will also appear at the very top of the Settings screen on your phone.

A data saver button may be added to the settings menu.

Avoid App Crashes When Wi-Fi Is Unavailable

For optimal performance, it may be necessary to leave certain programs and services running in the background even when you aren't actively using them. You may enable "Unrestricted data" for individual applications to allow them to use mobile data while running in the background.

1. Start the phone's configuration program.
2. Select "Network & Internet," followed by "Data Saver," "Unlimited Data," etc.
3. While Data Saver is active, launch the app or service that requires mobile data.

Adjust Nighttime Display Setting

Change the screen's color settings to conserve battery life and make the display more legible in low light. You may use your phone in the evening and have an easier time drifting off to sleep by switching to a Dark theme, Night Light, or Grayscale.

Android 9 or later is required for some of the instructions below.

Automatic Phone Backdrop
Your phone's backdrop and applications will dim automatically.

If you want a darker backdrop on your phone, choose the Dark theme. The Dark theme may be set to automatically activate at night.

The battery life of your phone will increase if you utilize applications that are compatible with the Dark theme. Battery life won't be improved by apps that don't support the Dark theme. If you disable location services, you will also lose the ability to schedule events from sunset to morning.

1. Start the phone's configuration program.

2. Select Display followed by Dark Theme.
3. The timetable for tapping.
4. Select a specific time, the hours between sunset and daybreak, or the evening hours before bed.

When using Bedtime mode, the Dark theme is automatically activated with Android 13 and later.

1. Start the phone's configuration program.
2. Select Display followed by Dark Theme.
3. Turns on automatically when the time is set to do so.

Tip: Selecting Schedule followed byNone will disable the automatic activation of the Dark theme.

To guarantee the appropriate operation of Bedtime mode:

1. Upgrade to version 3.0 of the Digital Health app immediately.
2. To get alerts about your digital health, activate the feature in your phone's settings.

Quick Settings on your phone include a dark theme, a night light, and a bedtime mode.

Automatically Decrease Wallpaper
Phone wallpaper brightness will decrease automatically.

You may reduce the brightness of your wallpaper at night on Android 13 and later.

1. Start the phone's configuration program.
2. Look at Digital Health and safety settings for kids.
3. Select the "Bedtime" setting.
4. Start the "Bedtime" setting.
5. Select Modify and then Choices for late-night viewing.
6. Dim the wallpaper by turning it on.

Set Your Display Automatically
Set your display to amber or night mode automatically.

You may adjust the amount of blue light your screen emits to make using your phone simpler in low light. It may be more challenging to nod off under blue illumination. Night Light is an app that lets you make your screen red or amber so that your eyes can more easily adapt to the dark.

1. Start the phone's configuration program.
2. Go to the Display menu, and then choose Night Light.
3. The schedule allows you to choose a time frame for your work.
   - Choose your own on/off time by selecting Turns on at the custom time. Next, specify a "Start time" and a "End time."
   - Just hit the "Turns on from sunset to sunrise" button. If you disable location services, the sunset-to-dawn timer won't operate.

To disable the automatic activation of night mode, choose Schedule, then None.

Turn To Screen Grayscale Instantly

Grayscale may convert your phone's display to black and white, which might help you relax before bed.

1. Start the phone's configuration program.
2. Look at Digital Health and safety settings for kids.
3. Select the "Bedtime" setting.
4. Initiate Nighttime Mode
   - To set a bedtime screen timeout on Android 13 and later, go to Settings > Display > Screen timeout.
5. Change to grayscale mode.

Quick Settings on your phone include a dark theme, a night light, and a bedtime mode.

Modify Your Theme

The themes may be toggled on and off whenever you choose, giving you complete control over the aesthetic.

1. Start the phone's configuration program.
2. Select Screen.
3. Select a hue from your device's display:
   - The dark theme may be activated in the "Appearance" menu.
   - Turn on Night Light in the "Color" menu.

Remotely Manage Your Pixel

The Pixel 4's Motion Sense feature may detect your presence. Gestures allow you to do tasks on your phone without needing to unlock the screen.

Motion Sense will not work when in Battery Saver or Airplane mode.

Adjust The Motion Detection
1. Launch the Settings app on your Pixel 4.
2. Motion Detection Followed by the Tap System.
3. Awaken Motion Detection.

After activating Motion Sense:

- At times, a faint blue tinge will appear at the display's peak. This light indicates that a shortcut gesture is ready for use, or that one has been used recently.
- Motion Sense detects your proximity but cannot identify you.
- A camera is not what Motion Sense is.
- Your phone does all the work for Motion Sense. Google does not get sensor signal data.

Make Swift Movements
Move rapidly and make swift movements.

Disruptions In The Silence
Wave over your phone to mute the microphone, cancel the timer, or reschedule the alarm.

1. Make use of a timer, alarm, or phone call.
2. Wave your hand over the screen once when it turns off.

Waving your hand over your phone will not silence your alarm or reject your call. Instead, when you reach for your phone, it snoozes the alarm, puts the call on hold, or lowers the volume.

Song Skipping
Wave your hand over the phone to skip songs or return to the last one you were listening to. Even if the music app isn't active or the screen is off, you can still use this gesture to control playback.

1. Put on some tunes on your smartphone.
2. You may advance to the next track by waving your hand from left to right in front of the phone.
3. Wave your hand from right to left over the phone to skip back to the previous track.

Start And Stop The Music

You can play and stop music by tapping the top of your phone. This default-disabled gesture may be used with the vast majority of music players.

When you start playing music on your phone:

- You may halt the music by tapping the screen above it.
- You may keep the music going by tapping the screen above it.

Alter Quick Gestures Settings
Activate your display when physically close.

When it detects you are nearby, your phone may display the clock and any new notifications.

1. Launch the Settings app on your Pixel 4.
2. Motion Detection Followed by the Tap System.
3. Filtering by "Ambient display":
   - If you activate Reach to check your phone, your display will light up when you reach for it.
   - Select "On when you're nearby" or "Always on" from the Idle lock screen menu to keep the screen active when you're close to it.

To begin or end blocking out noise

1. Launch the Settings app on your Pixel 4.
2. Motion Detection Followed by the Tap System.
3. You should press silence to mute any incoming calls or texts.
4. Disable or enable the Silence feature.

To stop skipping songs, swipe in a different direction.

1. Launch the Settings app on your Pixel 4.
2. Motion Detection Followed by the Tap System.

3. To skip songs, press.
   - Swipe direction may be altered with a touch.
   - Tap Skipping tracks to turn it off.

Motions For Problem-Solving

If a quick hand signal doesn't work:

- Take off the cover or screen protector from your phone. Make sure your case or screen protector doesn't interfere with the top of your display.
- Deactivate Motion Sense and activate it again.
- The phone has to be turned off and on again.
- Make sure you're located in a nation that allows the use of Motion Sense. In addition to the US and Canada, Motion Sense is also compatible with Singapore, Australia, Taiwan, Japan, and the majority of Europe. It won't function overseas if you visit a nation where its use is illegal.

Chapter Four
Put In And Take Calls

The Phone app, along with any other app or widget that displays your contacts, allows you to make and receive phone calls.

Almost often, you may just press a phone number and immediately begin dialing it. If you're using Google Chrome, you may be able to copy phone numbers that are highlighted by tapping on them.

You can get the Phone app from the Google Play Store if you don't already have it.

- Your mobile device isn't compatible with the Phone app if you're unable to install it.
- Follow the on-screen instructions after installing the app to make it your primary phone utility.

You must be running Android 7.0 or later to complete any of these tasks.

Put In A Call

You must choose to make the phone app your default when prompted.

1. The Phone app must be launched.
2. Choose a contact:
   - Select Dialpad to input a phone number.
   - Tap Contacts to choose a previously stored contact. Based on your past call log, we may provide you with a list of recommended call recipients.
   - Select Recents from the menu to see the most recently dialed numbers.
   - Select Favorites from the menu to choose a contact from your saved list.
3. Make a call by tapping.
4. Select End call after you're through talking. To make a call disappear, move the call bubble to the right side of the screen.

Some networks and devices even allow for video calls, video conferences, and real-time text (RTT) chats.

Take A Call Or Ignore It

The number or name of the person calling you appears on the screen when you receive a call. When Google can confirm a phone number, the word "Verified" will appear in the space above the relevant information.

- If your phone is locked and a call comes in, you may either touch Answer or slide the white circle to the top of the screen.
- When your phone is locked, swipe the white circle to the bottom of the screen or press the Dismiss button to end the call. Callers who are not accepted may leave a message.
- Swipe up on the new message button inside the Messages app to decline the call and instead compose a text message to the caller.

Tips:

- The call you are now on will be put on pause while you attend to the incoming call.
- If Google Assistant is active, you may use voice commands to accept or reject incoming calls. Tell Google to pick up the phone by saying, "Hey Google, answer the call."
- "Hey Google, just hang up on them."

Dial The Appropriate Numbers

When a call is in progress:

Select Dialpad to access the telephone keypad.

- Select Speaker to toggle between the earpiece, the speaker, and any Bluetooth headphones you may have paired.
- The Mute button mutes or unmutes your device's microphone.
- You may put a call on hold without really ending it by selecting Hold. Simply release Hold to resume the call.
- Customers who have opted into the catch phone service option are the only ones who may use this feature. In any other case, an error notice will be shown.

You may easily switch between active calls by tapping Switch. Others are delayed indefinitely.

- Select Call Merge to combine all active calls into a single conference call.
- The call may be put on hold by returning to the Home screen.
- You may drag the call bubble to reposition it.
- Drag the call bubble to the "Hide" location at the bottom of the screen to conceal it.
- When using certain plans and gadgets, you can:
- Attempt a video call instead. Select a video chat Communication through a video screen.
- Make a call forwarding request to another number:
  1. During a call, choose the Add Call option.
  2. Put in your number here.
  3. Make a call by tapping.
  4. Select Transfer after the call is connected. After Step 2, your call will be routed to the number you provided.

Use Wi-Fi For Phone Calls

It's possible to make calls through Wi-Fi rather than your cell provider in certain situations. Wi-Fi calling is not available from all service providers.

You'll need to enable this function in your settings before you can make calls via Wi-Fi.

You must be running Android 6.0 or later to complete any of these tasks.

Activate Wi-Fi Calling

Your cell service provider may charge you more to make calls when connected to their Wi-Fi network.

Use The Wi-Fi Calling Features

Make use of the Wi-Fi calling features provided by your cellular service provider.

1. Release the Phone program.
2. Select Settings by clicking More.
3. Phone Calls Recorded.
4. Select Wi-Fi calling. If you don't have this choice, it's because your network provider doesn't allow it.
   - Some providers enable Wi-Fi calling even if you don't have their service.
   - Even if your wireless provider doesn't facilitate Wi-Fi phone calls, you may still make and receive them using a VoIP service.

Make A Wireless Call

Wi-Fi calls are the same as any other call after you've set them up. The words "Internet Call" or "Wi-Fi calling" will appear on the alert screen whenever you are online.

Your cell provider will handle calls while you're not in the range of a Wi-Fi hotspot.

Message Retrieval Instructions

Simply dial the number provided by your voicemail provider and listen to your messages. The Phone app on certain smartphones and with some service providers will display a list of your voicemails.

You must be running Android 6.0 or later to complete any of these tasks.

Message Retrieving
Select a pop-up alert for a message

You may listen to your voicemail by tapping the notification on your phone.

1. Scroll down the screen by swiping down from the top.
2. Choose the Voicemail option.

Dial the number to your voicemail

Get in touch with your voicemail system to listen to your messages.

1. Release the Phone program.
2. Select Dialpad from the bottom options.
3. One-on-one contact 1.

Listen to messages in a list format in the Phone app.

Not all areas or service providers provide this option. You can use visual voicemail to:

- AT&T's Advice: If you want visible voicemail, be sure your data plan covers it. You may either check your current data plan or contact AT&T customer support to get this information.
- Cellcom Coriolis
- O2 Orange T-Mobile Google Fi

The visible voicemail functionality of the Phone app is disabled when you use the voicemail app provided by your mobile service provider.

Activate The Visual Voicemail
1. Release the Phone program.

2. Select More Choices More at the top right.
3. Select Voicemail from the Settings menu.
4. Install a visual voicemail system.

Tips:

- Voicemail transcription is a feature available on several devices and service providers.
- When you disable visual voicemail, the recordings will be removed from the Phone app, but your carrier may preserve a backup copy.

Use A Variety Of SIM Cards

Use a variety of SIM cards with visible voicemails.

Your device or service provider may not allow you to use visual voicemail with numerous SIM cards.

1. Release the Phone program.
2. Choose More in the upper right corner.
3. Select Voicemail from the Settings menu.
4. Use a SIM card reader.
5. Install a visual voicemail system.
6. Press the Back button in the upper left corner.
7. Swap out SIM cards.
8. Install a visual voicemail system.

Tips:

- Visual voicemail from each SIM card is presented in its tab.
- You may need to re-enable visual voicemail after switching data SIMs.
- Cache data is retained even when a SIM is removed, however, switching between SIMs is not possible. If you disable a SIM, its cached data will be removed and you won't be able to switch between SIMs in the browser.

Look At A Log Of Your Voicemails
Take a look at a log of your voicemails

1. Release the Phone program.

2. Click Voicemail at the very bottom. If you can't locate "Voicemail," just dial the number on your voicemail.

The voicemail may be expanded and the recording shared that way. Then, after sending, press Send again. Simply choose the desired app by tapping on it.

Examine a text version of your voicemails.

A voicemail transcription is available on several mobile devices and services. The following may be transcribed from voicemail:

- Charter and Verizon, Comcast and Verizon, O2 and Freedom, T-Mobile and Pixel, Tracfone and T-Mobile, and Visible and Verizon, all use the same network.

Obtainability varies by territory. Only Android 8.0 and later versions support transcription, and only in English and Spanish.

Start Transcribing Your Voicemails
1. Release the Phone program.
2. Select Additional Actions on the menu. Select Voicemail after clicking more, then Settings.
3. Start transcribing your voicemails.

Tips:

- If you use a compatible carrier or device but don't have the "Voicemail transcription" option, visual voicemail may help.
- Sharing a transcript is as simple as selecting the recipient, tapping Share, and then selecting the recipient's preferred app.
- When activated, Google will transcribe both new and old voicemails.
- Google utilizes automated voicemail transcribing systems that don't tie in with your Google Account. Your phone, and not Google, is where your voicemails will be kept.
- When voicemail transcription is off, both the recordings and the transcriptions are removed from the Phone app.
- To aid Google in developing better transcription tools, you may provide the company with transcripts and recordings of your voicemails. Your phone number and Google Account

information will not be revealed to anybody reviewing your donated voicemails.

Donate Voicemails To Be Transcribed
1. Release the Phone program.
2. Select Settings by clicking More Choices.
3. Activate the speech-to-text function in your voicemail.

Modify Your Voicemail Settings
1. Release the Phone program.
2. Select More Choices More at the top right.
3. Select Voicemail from the Settings menu.
4. Possibilities include:
    - You may swap out your voicemail provider: Select Service after selecting the More Preferences menu.
    - Put in place your voicemail system: Select Setup after selecting Advanced Settings.
    - Modify how you're notified: Select "Alerts" from the menu.
    - To activate the vibrating mode, turn on: Select Vibrate from the Notifications menu, followed by Advanced.

The Voicemail Alerts Are Broken

You may not get voicemail alerts or may receive garbled text messages from your carrier if you go from a phone that includes voicemail in the Phone app to one that does not.

If the Voicemail option is not available in the Phone app on your device:

Get In Touch With Your Cell Phone Company
Get in touch with your cell operator and request a reduction to the standard voicemail package.

Double-Check Your Voicemail's Settings.
1. Release the Phone program.
2. Select More Choices More at the top right.
3. Select Voicemail followed by Advanced Settings from the Settings menu.
4. Select "Your carrier" under "Service."

Modify Phone Preferences

You have control over the phone's ringtone, vibration, rapid response, and call log settings.

You must be running Android 7.0 or later to complete any of these tasks.

The Volume & Vibration Level
1. Release the Phone program.
2. Select Settings by clicking More.
3. Tonal and vibratory taps.
   - Select Ringtone > Available tones to listen to and select one.
   - Choose the option to have your phone vibrate as well for incoming calls.
   - Dial-pad tones allow you to play sounds whenever you touch the dial-pad. (If you don't see "Dial pad tones," then choose "Keypad tones.")

Alter The Caller Id Display
Modify the way the names of callers are displayed.

Not all languages allow you to alter caller ID names.

1. Release the Phone program.
2. Select Settings by clicking More.
3. Select Viewing Options.
   - You may choose how your phone stores your call log by tapping the Sort by button.
   - Select Name format to alter how the phone displays names in the call log.

Alter Your Text-Based Replies
When you can't talk right now, an automated text message is the next best thing. How to customize your auto-replies through text messages:

1. Release the Phone program.
2. Select Settings by clicking More.
3. Select the Quick options.
4. Select a suitable answer by tapping it.

5. Modify the answer.
6. Tap Ok.

Modify More Parameters

Make phone calls using a TTY or RTT.

If you want to be able to text during phone calls:

1. Release the Phone program.
2. Choose Preferences by selecting More.
3. Select the appropriate accessibility settings.
4. Tap Real-time text (RTT) to see your RTT preferences.
   - You may conceal the calling button while still accepting incoming RTT calls by tapping Not visible.
   - If you want the RTT button to be visible during a call, choose that option.
   - Select Always Visible to permanently display the RTT button.

Text Telephone (TTY) mode is an alternative to RTT for phones that don't have it. Text Telephone mode may be activated in a few different ways.

- Select "TTY Off" to use the phone's audio and microphone without text input.
- Select TTY Full to make use of written text in both directions.
- Select TTY HCO to have your input text read aloud by the other party.
- Select TTY VCO to have your voice heard while reading the other person's response in text format.

Check with your provider to see whether TTY or RTT capabilities are included in your phone package.

Stop searching for locations near you

If you want to utilize the Phone app's built-in search function to find local businesses, you'll need to allow it to access your location.

1. Release the Phone program.
2. Select More, then Settings, and finally nearby locations.
3. To see what's close by, choose it at the top of the screen.

If you notice "Location permission is denied" under "Google Account," touch it.

While away, have someone assist you make phone calls.

Move To A New Nation
In the Phone app, your default country is determined by your phone number. If you want to move countries:

1. Release the Phone program.
2. Select "More," "Settings," "Calls," and "Assisted dialing."
3. Select your default nation.
4. Select a nation.
5. Pick the Save option.

Don't Keep Tacking On Country Codes
1. Release the Phone program.
2. Select "More," "Settings," "Calls," and "Assisted dialing."
3. Switch off the feature that helps you dial.

Adjust the setting for Clear Calling.

Both the Pixel 7 and the Pixel 7 Pro have this capability.

The availability of this function during a call is contingent on the bandwidth available during that call.

1. Launch the device's configuration menu.
2. Select Clear Calling after tapping Sound & Vibration.
3. Turn Clear Calling on or off as needed.

See & Erase Call Logs
A log of your incoming, outgoing, and missed calls is shown. You may also remove unwanted calls from that log.

You must be running Android 6.0 or later to complete any of these tasks.

View Your Phone's Call Log
1. Launch the phone application.
2. Select Recently Used.
3. Each call in your list will be represented by one of these icons:

- Calls not answered (incoming) ignored call
- Returned (unsolicited) calls An Incoming Call
- Incoming and outgoing calls made by you

View Contact Info
Tap the call in your history, and then tap Call details, to get further information about that call.

The time, duration, and direction of each incoming and departing call to that number will be shown.

Use Address Book
Put phone numbers in your address book.

Simply touch the call and choose "Add to Contacts" to save the number from your call log. Compose a new contact or add to an existing one.

Get Rid Of Your Call Logs
Take a call off your record

1. Launch the phone application.
2. Select Recently Used.
3. Select a contact or phone number by tapping on it.
4. Select the Call Information option.
5. Select Delete Trash from the menu bar.

Eliminate any traces of your past calls.

1. Launch the phone application.
2. Select Recently Used.
3. Select More More, and then Conversation Logs.
4. Select More More, and then Get rid of old call logs.
5. To permanently remove your call log, choose Ok when prompted.

Spam Blockers And Caller ID
Put in place spam blockers and caller IDs.

Caller ID and spam prevention features allow you to learn more about unknown callers and get alerts about suspected spam calls while making or receiving calls.

Your phone may share call data with Google so features like caller ID and spam prevention may function.

Calls from numbers not in your contact list are routed to Google so that the company may use the number to verify the identity of the caller or block unwanted calls.

Your Google Contacts are not shared with the company.

You must be running Android 6.0 or later to complete any of these tasks.

Activate/Deactivate Caller ID

Activate or deactivate caller ID and spam filtering Caller ID and spam filtering are enabled by default. Putting it to sleep is an option.

Your phone may share call data with Google so features like caller ID and spam prevention may function. It does not affect whether or not your phone number is shown when you make a call.

1. Launch the phone application on your gadget.
2. Select Additional Actions on the menu. Select Spam and Call Blocking under Settings after clicking More.
3. Turn Access spam and caller ID.
4. Optional: To stop unwanted calls from reaching your phone, use the setting "Filter spam calls." Even though you won't be notified of missed calls or voicemails, you'll be able to go through your call log to see which ones were filtered out.

Businesses having a Google My Business listing will appear in the caller ID menu on Google phones. It also checks for calls made from work or school numbers against the local phone book. The caller ID system may classify businesses.

Get in touch with your institution's administration to get your login name changed.

Changing your company's name or phone number? It's time to update your company details.

Put On The Caller ID Message

Turn on the Caller ID announcement to hear the caller's number and name spoken.

1. Launch the phone application on your gadget.
2. Select Additional Actions on the menu. Click "More," then "Settings," then "Caller ID Announcement," and finally "Caller ID." Play the number that is calling.
3. Just choose one...
   - Always
   - Only when headphones are involved
   - Never

Report A Spammer

Mark calls as spam you may block calls from a certain number and even report the spammer if you often receive unwanted calls from them.

1. Launch the phone application on your gadget.
2. Select Recents from the drop-down menu.
3. To report a call as spam, just tap on it.
4. Choose a spam filter or report it.

If you wish to report a call as spam, you may do so by tapping and holding the call. Choose between blocking and reporting spam.

Spot the spam

You should assume that a call labeled "Suspected spam caller" or "Spam" is spam. You have the option of picking up or rejecting and reporting the caller.

Please inform us of any spam filtering errors.

You may file a complaint if a call from a friend or family member is mistakenly labeled as spam. Your phone will no longer flag calls from this number as spam if you answer them in the future.

1. Launch the phone application on your gadget.
2. Select the Recent calls option.
3. Ignorantly marked as spam? Tap that call.
4. Select Unblock from the menu.

Caller Id Verification / Sharing

Information about companies that phone you or those you make calls to may now be shared. This data may be used to:

- Put in a company or product classification.
- Appear during phone talks
- Share information about your company, institution, or group to help others become involved.

A caller ID might be confirmed or a new one suggested.

1. Launch the phone application on your gadget.
2. Select Recents from the drop-down menu.
3. Tap A company, perhaps? Get a response from your Caller ID, then proceed as directed.
4. Activate the Send button.
   - If the phone number isn't a certified business line, Google won't get any of your private data.
   - Your submission will not be linked to any identifying details.

After providing input, if you decide to modify your preference:

1. Select the call you wish to utilize by touching and holding it in the Recents menu.
2. Choose to Submit a comment.

Block & Unblock A Caller
A phone number may be blocked or unblocked.

You may block a number if you don't want to receive calls from that number. Your phone will automatically reject calls from that number.

You must be running Android 6.0 or later to complete any of these tasks.

Hide A Phone Number

1. Launch the app on your phone.
2. Select Call Record from the menu that appears.
3. To block a number, just accept a call from it and tap the call.
4. Select Spam Reporting / Blocking.

Blocked callers cannot leave voicemails if visible voicemail is enabled.

Filter Out Random Numbers
1. Launch the app on your phone.
2. Click on More.
3. Choose the Numbers you've blocked by tapping Settings.
4. Make use of Unknown.

Calls from unknown or private numbers will be blocked. Calls from numbers that aren't saved in your contacts list will still come through.

Remove A Call Block
1. Launch the app on your phone.
2. Click on More.
3. Choose the Numbers you've blocked by tapping Settings.
4. To remove a block from a certain number, select it and then press Clear Clear and Unblock.

Your call history will not reflect any incoming calls from the blocked number while it was active.

Call Screening & Answering
Check who's calling before picking up the phone.

Before answering a call, you may utilize Call Screen to see who it is and why they are calling. Call Screen operates independently of wireless networks and cellular data. Google Assistant calls that are answered use up your allotted carrier minutes.

Locations That Offer Call Screen
All Pixel phones in the US include an automated call-screening feature.

Pixel phones in the following regions allow users to manually filter incoming calls:

- Australia
- Canada
- France Germany

- Ireland
- Italy
- Japan
- Spain
- UK US

In the US and Canada, you may use the Manual Call Screen on certain Android smartphones.

Only SIM cards from countries where Call Screen is accessible will operate with the manual Call Screen feature.

Prepare For Instant Call Filtering

Call Screen is incompatible with any other call recording or screen recording applications. To get the most out of Call Screen, disable these programs first.

1. Verify that your Phone app is up to date. Select update if it appears.
2. Release the Phone program.
3. Select the More buttons, followed by Settings, and finally the Spam and Calls screen.
4. Turn on the feature to see the caller and spam ID.
5. To access the call screen, press.
6. In the menu that appears, choose "Unknown call settings," then add the caller categories you'd want to filter.
7. Select the option to automatically filter for inappropriate content. Just ignore those automated phone calls. If not, your options are:
   - Toll the phone
   - Check-in mechanically. Just ignore those automated phone calls.
   - Subtly back down
8. Optional: Save Call Screen audio allows you to record incoming and outgoing filtered calls.
   - With the option to "Save Call Screen audio," just the caller's voice will be saved. Your phone doesn't record the audio it plays to callers. Your call will not be recorded if you choose to answer.

Automatically Screen Calls

Your phone won't automatically filter calls if you're using headphones or Bluetooth.

1. Start the screen going on autopilot. Just ignore those automated phone calls.
2. A quiet "Screening an unknown call" alert will play whenever a call is being screened.
   - Optional: Swipe down on the alert to see the options to answer or decline the call.
3. Your Google Assistant picks up the phone and inquires as to the caller's identity and purpose.
   - Your phone will automatically end the call if the Assistant identifies it as spam or robocall.
   - Your phone will ring and display the caller's response if the Assistant decides that it is not a robocall or spam call.
   - While the call is being screened, your phone will pause all media playback, including videos and music.

Calls Are Manually Screened

1. To ignore a call, choose the Screen Call option.
2. Your Google Assistant will first see who is calling and why before letting you answer. The caller's response will be transcribed instantly.
3. After the caller answers, you have the option to pick up, ignore, or end the conversation. The caller hears the following responses:
   - Is it a crisis? "Are you in dire need of contacting them?"
   - Send to spam: Take remove my name and phone from your mailing and calling lists immediately. Adieu and thank you.
   - I'll get back to you ASAP. They are unable to do so at this time but will call you back when they can. Adieu and thank you.
   - It's tough to make out what you're saying right now, and I don't know why. Could you just repeat that?"

No Manual Call Screening Option

Additional actions may be required to activate the Call filter if you are unable to manually filter calls.

1. Release the Phone program.
2. To change the call screen, go to More More > Settings > Call Screen.
3. Just follow the on-screen prompts to configure Call Screen.
   - If there are no on-screen instructions, Call Screen is not compatible with your smartphone.

Collect Call Transcripts & Recordings

A transcript of all call screenings will be stored on your phone. Your Pixel phone may also act as a recording device.

1. Activate the recording of the call screen.
2. Release the Phone program.
3. Select Recently Used from the menu.
4. Select the call that has been previewed.
5. Choose either the Transcript or the Transcript with audio. Tap History, then See Transcript if you don't see those choices.
6. Optional: If you tap and hold the screened call, you may erase both the transcript and the recording. Click the Delete button.

The Function Of The Call Screen

- The people you know are what the Call filter uses to decide whether it should filter a call. You may avoid screening for a certain number by adding it as a contact.
- Google's spam database may help your phone identify robocalls and other unwanted calls. On the other hand, not all robocalls and spam calls can be identified.
- You may prevent your phone from saving information about screened calls to your Google Account, Google Assistant Activity page, or Web and App Activity by using the Call Screen feature.
- Don't utilize auto-screening for incoming calls if you forward calls. We do not forward screened calls.
- The call Screen may not always accurately capture what was spoken during a call.

Multitask & Share Applications

You can multitask and share applications while on the phone.

While multitasking on your phone, you may keep your Google Duo video chat going in a little window using picture-in-picture (PIP). During a call, you have the option of sharing your screen to play films or exhibit images.

These capabilities are not accessible till Android version 8.

Insert Images Inside Images
1. Closed Pair.
2. Get a video chat going.
3. Select "Home" from the menu.
   - If you're using Android 8.0 or later, the Duo call will keep working.
   - Your video will halt, but the audio will continue to play if your device doesn't support PIP.

Take Out The Overlays
When you get a call, picture-in-picture mode will exit.

- To make the call full screen, double-tap the PIP window.
- Get off the phone.
- To dismiss the PIP window, choose Close Close.
- Launch a new program in full-screen mode. There will be no pause in the video call.

If you're using Duo, disable PIP.

1. Launch the device's configuration menu.
2. Select Picture-in-picture by going to Apps & notifications > Advanced > Special app access > Picture-in-picture.
3. The Two-Handed Tap.
4. Stop allowing picture-in-picture mode.

Cast Your Screen
You will not be seen by the camera throughout the screen-sharing process. Only in one-on-one calls may you use the screen-sharing feature.

1. Launch Google's Duo app.
2. Gets a video chat going.

3. Scroll down and choose More choices More, then Screen sharing, and finally Start Immediately.
   - The other caller has the option to share their screen with you as well.
4. Select Screen Share to stop the screen-sharing session.

If you can't locate the Screen sharing option, try tapping More and swiping to the left.

Live sharing allows you to choose and launch applications on your Samsung S22, S8, or Pixel smartphone.

- Control the sharing of your screen collaboratively.

Utilize Direct My Call

Direct My Call is an app that displays a virtual telephone keypad and an on-screen menu when you dial the number of a company that uses an automated menu system. You may choose an item from the menu by tapping its corresponding button.

- On Pixel 4a and later, you may be presented with menu items before they are uttered when on a call.
- By default, your device's "Faster menu options" setting will be on.
- You may disable Direct My Call by selecting More More > Settings > Direct My Call from the Phone menu. Disabling "Faster menu options" will do the trick.

Verify Everything You Need
Make sure you have everything you need.

To use Direct My Call, you must:

- Across the pond
- For the English version, on Pixel 3a and later devices
- When using the most recent update to the Phone app,

Activate / Disable Direct My Call
1. Release the Phone program
2. Select More in the upper right, and then press Settings.
3. Just use the "Direct My Call" button.

4. Adjust the setting for Direct My Call.

A current phone call may be ended by tapping the Close button in the upper left corner of the screen.

Distribute Your Call Logs
Disseminate information gleaned from your conversation.

Once you hit "send," there's no turning back.

Share your call recording and transcript afterward to help us fine-tune Direct My Call.

1. Release the Phone program.
2. Select Recently Used at the very end.
3. Tap the "Help us improve this" button that appears underneath the call log entry, then "Continue," then "Continue."
4. The text field for your comments is optional.
5. Select Send in the upper right corner.

To send information without disclosing your email address, hit the Down arrow next to the "From" section on the Send Feedback page, and then select Google User.

Chapter Five
Learn How To Use Messages

A message is a messaging app that allows you to send and receive text, images, voice memos, and video. Google Play has Messages available for download if you don't already have it.

Change Your Primary Message App
Change your primary messaging app to Messages.

You must be running Android 6.0 or later to complete any of these tasks.

Other applications may be able to access your SMS messages if you keep them in the device's SMS database. Talk to your device's maker if you need help learning how to modify app permissions.

Messages may be set as the default messaging app on an iOS device if there are many options. If you've set Messages as your preferred messaging app, you can only send and receive new text messages via Messages, and you can only see your text message history in Messages.

Choose an alternative to make Messages your default messaging app:

1. The Messages app must be opened.
2. Follow the on-screen prompts to change the default messaging app.

Alternatively:

1. Initiate the configurations menu.
2. Just go to Apps.
3. Select Messages from the app drawer, followed by SMS, and finally Messages.

You may change the default messaging app on your iPhone to anything else, or you can delete the Messages app entirely.

Reach Out To A Contact
Reach out to a contact and start chatting.

The Messages app will recognize a contact if it already exists on your phone. A new contact may be added without leaving the app.

1. The Messages app must be opened.
2. Select the Chat Now button.
3. Type the recipient's full name, phone number, or email address.
4. Once you're done typing, hit the button.

Enter A Phone Number

Create a new contact in your discussion list by entering a phone number.

1. The Messages app must be opened.
2. Pick an ongoing chat with someone who isn't in your address book.
3. Select More, then Add Contact from the menu.

Create A New Contact

Create a new contact directly from a chat.

1. The Messages app must be opened.
2. To add a contact to your phonebook, find a group chat that includes the desired number and choose it.
3. Select the menu icon, then choose Details.
4. Select the desired contact's number and tap the Add contact button.

Modify Who Receives Alerts

1. The Messages app must be opened.
2. Start a new discussion with the individual whose alert settings you need to modify.
3. Select "More," "Details," and "Notifications" from the menu that appears.

You have the option to entirely disable or enable notifications for this individual, as well as modify the display settings for notifications.

Reject A Connection

If you block a contact, you will no longer hear from them or see any of their communications.

1. The Messages app must be opened.
2. The best way to block someone is to start talking to them.
3. Select More, then Details, and finally More. Stop spam and report it.
4. The option to also report spam is available.

Communicate By Text / Voice
Use Messages to communicate by text or voice.

Using Messages, you may communicate with your contacts and pals through text messages.

You must be running Android 6.0 or later to complete any of these tasks.

Kick Off A Discussion
1. The Messages app must be opened.
2. If you want to compose anything, click the compose button.
3. Under "To," provide the names, phone numbers, or email addresses of the people you want to contact. You are not limited to only selecting from your most often used contacts.

Message Someone
1. Select the text field and tap it.
2. Type your message here. You may hit Back Back to store it as a draft and return it later.
3. To finish, press the Send Send button.

Leave A Voicemail
1. Select the text field and tap it.
2. Strike the Microphone.
3. Put together a voicemail.
   - You may preview the audio message before sending it since it is preserved as a draft.
   - Once you press the Send Send button, the voice message will be sent.
4. Then, you should press the send button.

Check Out The Recorded

You may either listen to a voicemail or read a transcript of it when one is delivered to you.

1. The Messages app must be opened.
2. Listen to the voicemail in the conversation you got it in.
3. Select View transcript at the top of the voicemail.

Send On A Message

You may copy in a new recipient at any point after starting a chat.

1. The Messages app must be opened.
2. Start a conversation.
3. Select and hold a message with a tap.
4. Click "More" and then "Next."
5. Pick a communicator.
6. Then, you should press the send button.

Skim Your Text Messages

Swipe down from the top of the screen and choose New Message to read a new message. Here's an updated message.

You may reread any Messages thread at any time.

- Set the read status on all messages: To mark everything as read, choose More More.
- Play a recording or video: Listen in on a chat. Select Play Play next to the media file you want to play.
- Dial a number: Listen in on a chat. Select Call Call in the upper right corner.
- Check out old email archives: To see archived discussions, choose More More from the conversation list.

Images, Videos & Audio Sharing

Use Messages to share media such as images, videos, and audio.

You may use Messages to send and receive multimedia messages (MMS) such as images, videos, audio files, and GIFs.

- Some procedures need Android 6.0 or later.

- Give Messages access to transmit and receive files. Manage the access levels of your apps.

Sending Media
Send media (images, video, files, GIFs).

1. The Messages app must be opened.
2. Start a discussion or dialogue.
3. Just hit the "Add Attachment" button.
4. Pick a file to open.
5. Then, you should press the send button.

Media captured with Android Messages won't be stored locally.

Send Movies In Messages
Send clearer movies in Messages with the help of Google Photos.

Get the Google Photos app set up on your device first.

1. Join Chevron Messages on Google Photos.
2. Share a photo album from Google over iMessage.
- Even if the videos you wish to send aren't in Google Photos, Messages may generate a link to them.
- Those who have the album's URL may watch the videos inside it.
- If you and a friend are using partner sharing, both of you will be able to watch the videos you send each other via Messages.
1. Launch the messaging program.
2. Initiate a mobile texting or MMS conversation.
3. Select a photo or a gallery to attach it.
4. Choose the clip you wish to share.
   - A single link is generated even if numerous videos are chosen.
5. Select Add in the "Google Photos link" field.
   - To always send attachments as Google Photos links, choose the option always.
6. You should press the send button.
   - You may prevent a link from being delivered to Messages by tapping Cancel first. Even if you turn off Backup & sync, your videos will still be saved in Google Photos.

Tips:

- File sizes for attachments that aren't already in your Google Photos library may be previewed before they're uploaded.
- While your Google Photos links are being uploaded, produced, and delivered, you are free to work on other communications.
- Sharing a link to a media file will automatically add information about the file, such as the video's location, to your Google Photos album.

Check out the photo albums on Google

All Google Photos URLs you send using Messages are accessible to you.

1. Launch the messaging program.
2. In the upper right, choose more settings. Chevron Preferences Photos via Google.
3. You may access, edit, and remove shared links in Google Photos by selecting Manage Links.

The Results of Sharing

- By clicking "Send" in Google Photos, you can:
- Your contacts will get a push notice from the app as well as an in-app alert when you share anything with them. The shared item(s) will now be seen in their Sharing section.
- They will get an email telling them about the new album or discussion you shared with them.
- Until they see the album or chat, their account profile picture or initials will look faded.
- Viewing an album or chat will show the user's profile picture or initials next to the most recently viewed photographs, comments, and likes.
- Their account photo or initials will replace the default profile picture when they join a shared album or like, comment, or upload photographs to a shared album or chat.
- Your profile picture or initials will be shown next to the most recent images you've uploaded to an album or a discussion.

- If you upload a video shot in slow motion, your viewers may be able to adjust the pace of the movie to their liking.

Troubleshoot Images from Google

- Update your Google Photos and Messages to the newest versions.
- Verify that your mobile data or Wi-Fi connection is active.
- If the upload is taking too long, try a different connection or shrink the file.
- If a video is playing as you transmit it, the receiver will be alerted to the fact that it is playing.

Verbal Communication
1. The Messages app must be opened.
2. Start a discussion or dialogue.
3. Simply press and hold the microphone button.
4. Put your message on the record.
5. Select the "Send" button.

Swipe left on the conversation or shut the message to end a voice message.

Send In Your Coordinates
1. The Messages app must be opened.
2. Start a discussion or dialogue.
3. Dot the I and t. Location of Chevron Send

Modify Message Alerts & Preferences
You may choose to be alerted of new messages via:

- Sound Vibration Reminder
- You have the option of also:
- Images and videos from your device are being sent.

A message is capable of complex operations.

Android 8.0 or later is required for some of the instructions below.

Modify Worldwide Preferences
Modify the default settings for alerts

1. The Messages app must be opened.
2. Press the More button and then Settings.
    - Put an end to app notifications: Select Alerts, then. Disable any "Default settings" alerts.
    - Use Messages to send alerts to your mobile device: Select Alerts, then toggle On for Received Messages.
    - You may turn off message alert sounds by Mute Send Sound on Outgoing Messages.

Default messaging apps may be changed.

1. Launch the Settings application on your smartphone.
2. Select the SMS app by going to Apps, then Default Apps.

Format Text Size

You may adjust the text size by:

1. Launch the device's configuration utility.
2. Choose Text and display under Accessibility.
3. Decide on font size.
4. Adjust the text size with the slider.

Resize The Screen

Adjust the size of the text and images on your screen by:

1. Launch the device's configuration utility.
2. Go to Settings Accessibility and Words and screens and then Measurement on display.
3. You may adjust the screen's resolution using the slider.

Modify The Intricate Options

Modify how Messages transmits media assets like photos and music.

1. The Messages app must be opened.
2. Select Advanced by clicking the More button, followed by Settings.
    - Separately communicate with each participant in a discussion by sending a message or file: Select the chat room and then send a bulk text message with a personalized response to each recipient's phone.

Download attachments from emails mechanically: Enable MMS to download at no cost.
- Files may be downloaded on a roaming basis automatically: Enable MMS auto-downloading when traveling.

Send files using just alphabetic and numeric characters.

1. The Messages app must be opened.
2. Select Advanced by clicking the More button, followed by Settings.
   - Replace complex symbols with their basic equivalents: Switch on Simplify your character set.
   - Swap out your current file-transfer phone number with a new one: Select Contact number.

Modify your pop-up alert settings

Notification bubbles help keep ongoing discussions at hand. Pinning conversation bubbles to the home screen makes accessing messages from your connections easier.

1. The Messages app must be opened.
2. Select Additional Actions on the menu. Even farther, then Arrangements, and then Bubbles.
3. Choose:
   - Follow every discussion with alerts: Tap Everyone is free to speak their opinions.
   - Get alerts on certain people: Certain discussions may "bubble" if you tap.
   - Disable any alerts: Tap There will be no bubbling.

Tips:

- Modify each contact bubble settings: Start a chat and then Select Notifications from the menu that appears after selecting more.
- Delete a message: Drag the bubble down by touching and holding on to it.

New settings for alerts, banning, and group chats

1. The Messages app must be opened.

2. Launch a one-on-one chat or a group chat.
3. Select Additional Actions on the menu. Additional Information / Further Selections Details about the Group are below.
   - Put an end to all message alerts: Select Silent from the Notifications menu.
   - Get high-priority alerts: Select Priority from the Notifications menu.
   - Do not allow calls or texts from that number or that group: Select Spam and tap on Block & Report it.
   Select the "Report Spam" checkbox if you want to submit a spam report.
   - Include other individuals in the discussion: Select the +People button.

Website link previews should be disabled.

You have the option of enabling or disabling site-wide link previews:

1. The Messages app must be opened.
2. In the upper right, choose More Settings. Simply click "More," "Settings," and "Automatic Previews" to get started.
3. Please disable the preview display.
   - Select Show only web link previews to restrict previews to just links sent or received in a chat.

A word of advice: only share reliable links. Personal information such as a street address or account number may be included in a URL.

Dim the lights, please.

Only Android 10 and higher will be supported by these instructions.

1. Launch the Settings application on your smartphone.
2. Select Screen.
3. Toggle the use of the dark theme.

Deactivate the Verified SMS feature

Not all countries or areas support Verified SMS.

When turned on, Google checks SMS texts from verified companies.

Cancel your verifiable SMS:

1. The Messages app must be opened.
2. Select Additional Actions on the menu. Click "More," "Settings," then "Verified SMS."
3. Disable the option to confirm business senders.

Use Pixel's Emoji References

The emojis you want to use in your text will be offered when you utilize voice dictation. Even if you don't know the precise name of an emoji, you may still search for it.

Needed Items

The Pixel 7 and Pixel 7 Pro are the only Pixel devices that support suggested emojis. Pixel 6 and later are required for Assistant voice typing. You must have Google Assistant running to utilize the voice-to-text feature.

All areas now provide German and English for suggested emojis.

Insert Appropriate Emojis

With voice dictation, you can find any emoji without knowing its actual name. To enter a "happy emoji" or "excited emoji," for instance, just pronounce the word, and the appropriate emoji will be used. When a precise match isn't available, suggestions will be given on which to choose.

1. Launch a text-entry app on your Pixel phone.
2. To use voice recognition to input an emoji, click the microphone icon in the upper right corner of your keyboard.
3. Your message will now include the emoji you selected.

Gboard requires access to your microphone if you haven't used it previously. When the prompt appears, choose either While using the app or Only this time to authorize recording.

Indicative Emojis

Previously, clever dictation could insert an emoji into your text only by hearing its name. This update will recommend appropriate emojis for your recently dictated words.

Chapter Six
Use A Pixel Search Features
Use a Pixel phone's search, launch, and shut features

You can locate some of your applications on the Home screens, while the rest may be found under all applications. Apps may be launched, toggled, and simultaneously located.

How to Search for and Launch Applications

From Any Location
1. Use an upward swiping motion to get to the top of the screen.
2. To launch a specific app, just tap its icon.

You can discover your applications for school or work under the "Work" page of your Google Account.

In the wake of shortcuts
1. Tap and hold the app until it begins to respond to your touch.
2. Pick a path if many exist.

Start At The Beginning
1. Use an upward swiping motion to get to the top of the screen.
2. Simply put the app's name into the Search box to launch it.

Toggle between recently used applications

1. You have to swipe up from the bottom, hold, and then release.
   - If you're using Android Go and only have access to three buttons, choose recent applications.
2. The desired app may be accessed by swiping to the left or right.
3. To launch a specific app, just tap its icon.

Move the Home button to the right to make the change.

Done with applications

- Swipe up from the bottom, hold, and release to close a single app. Using the app, swipe up.
- A bottom-up swipe, held, will force close all open applications. Use a left-to-right swipe motion. Select Clear All on the left.

- Android app killing Go: Select, hold, then release the bottom finger to swipe up. Select Clear All from the bottom menu.
- Locate the Home button: Launch the main menu. Master the ins and outs of mobile navigation.
- You must disable background app processing.
  1. Swipe down twice from the screen's top to access Quick Settings.
  2. Tap # active applications (located in the bottom left) to see the number of currently running apps.
     - Alternatively, you may access the settings and power menus by tapping the corresponding numbers in the bottom right.
  3. Select "Stop" to end all running programs.

It is not necessary to shut down applications to save memory or battery life. Android handles this on its own.

Update your applications

Google Play is where you may find other applications.

Google's Pixel App Downloads

Google Play offers both free and paid applications for your Android device. While Google Play is our preferred app store, there are other options available.

There is a safety feature (Google Play Protect) on your phone that scans for malicious software, issues warnings, and deletes offending programs if required.

Android 8.0 or later is required for some of the instructions below.

Get Apps With Google Play

1. Startup Google Play.
   - Get the Google Play app from the app store on your mobile device.
   - Visit play.google.com from your PC.
2. Obtain a program that suits your needs.
3. Verify the app's trustworthiness by reading reviews written by users.

- The number of downloads and the star rating may be seen under the app's name.
- Just scroll down to the "Reviews" section to read the reviews.
4. Select the app you want to use, and then either press Install (for free applications) or the app's pricing.

Send problematic applications to Google Play's attention.

Please let us know about any app you see that you believe may be dangerous.

Get Third-Party Applications

Untrusted app stores pose a security risk to your device and data if you install such programs.

- Your phone is vulnerable to harm and data loss.
- Your privacy might be violated or compromised.

Use third-party app stores

1. Start the app's download on the other device.
2. Just do what it says on the screen. It may be necessary to choose Ok And then Install depending on the origin.
3. Tap Settings on the pop-up notification that appears.
4. Change the setting to Allow.

Stop the app from downloading from unknown sources.

1. Start the phone's configuration program.
2. Select applications > Special app access > Install unknown applications.
3. Select the program that you don't want to prompt you to install third-party software.
4. You should disable Allow for this source.

Assist Google in blocking malware from third-party app stores

Your phone may share information about applications installed from sources other than Google Play.

Google may use this data to improve its defenses against malicious software. This data may comprise server logs, app-related URLs, device ID, Android version, and IP address.

Alter / Reset A Default Software

You may set a default app in situations when many apps provide the same function. If you have many photo editing programs installed, you may choose one to launch when opening a picture.

Android 9 or later is required for some of the instructions below.

Changing The Defaults
Appearances are Defaults: Changing the Defaults

Responding to a request for a selection

1. When prompted, choose the desired app from your phone's menu.
2. Choose whether you wish to use that app permanently or just this once to do this task.
3. Your phone will no longer prompt you to choose an app before performing a task. You may reset the default to force your phone to ask again.

Take your pick

1. Start the phone's configuration program.
2. Select Apps, then Default Apps.
3. Select the default that should be altered and tap it.
4. Select the app you'd want to launch automatically.

Reset Apps Factory Settings

1. Start the phone's configuration program.
2. Mobile Apps.
3. Select the program you wish to make the default and then tap it again. Click See all applications or App details first to see whether it is there.
4. Click the open button.
5. Close all compatible link windows.

When you undo the default action, your phone will prompt you to choose an app the next time you do it.

Alter Access Settings For Apps

Some applications may need permission to access your phone's camera or contacts. A notice will appear, asking if you'd want to allow the app to use certain aspects of your phone. The Settings menu on your phone also allows you to modify app permissions on a per-app or per-permission basis.

Some of these instructions need Android 11 or later.

Modify Access Levels In Apps

1. Launch the phone's Settings menu.
2. Mobile Apps.
3. You may modify an app by tapping it. If you still can't locate it, choose See All Applications. Pick an app to use.
4. Have the Right to Tap.
    - Here you can see the permissions you granted or revoked for the app.
5. Permissions may be adjusted by tapping the item in question and then selecting Allow or Don't Allow.

You may have the following options for granting access to your location, cameras, and microphones:

- Constantly (Place only): The program is free to utilize the permission whenever it wants, even if you aren't currently interacting with it.
- This permission is app-specific. Only at that time may the app make use of the permission.
- Constantly inquire: This permission will be requested each time you launch the app. This app has permission to use your location until you close it.
- Please don't: Even if you're using the app, you won't be able to access the option.

Modify Access On Data Type

Find out what other applications share your current permission level. You can, for instance, see which programs can access your calendar.

1. Launch the phone's Settings menu.
2. Select the "Permission Manager" option under "Privacy".
3. Select a category of access.
   - The applications for which you granted or revoked permission will be shown here.
4. Select the app you want to modify the permissions for, then press the gear icon.

Classes Of Authorizations

Mobile device settings may vary. Get in touch with the product's maker for further information.

What each app permits when enabled is detailed below.

- Sensor data about your body's vitals are now available.
- Timekeeping: Make use of the pre-set timetable.
- You may see and edit your call logs here.
- Take images or record videos using your camera.
- Contacts: View your list of available contacts.
- Gets the current position of the device.
- Capture sound using the microphone.
- Bluetooth devices in the vicinity: programs may automatically scan for and pair with available devices.
- Manage and make calls through the telephone.
- Learn more about your physical activity by tracking your steps, distance, and time spent walking or riding.
- Read and send text messages using a short messaging service (SMS).
- Get somewhere to save your pictures and other data.
- Use the images, videos, and other material stored on your mobile device.

Disable Access
Disable access for inactive applications automatically

1. Launch the phone's Settings menu.
2. Mobile Apps.
3. You may modify an app by tapping it.
   - If you still can't locate it, choose See All Applications. Pick an app to use.
4. In the menu that appears, choose "Unused app settings," and then select "Pause app activity if unused."

Join Google Apps To Your Profile

In your Google Account, you may set preferences for how your applications will sync your most recent messages, emails, and other data.

Android 9 or later is required for some of the instructions below.

Definition Of Sync's Effects

When your phone is synced, the information in your Google applications is updated and you are notified of any changes.

Which Applications Share Data

All of your Google-made applications will sync to your Google Account without you having to do a thing. Google's applications each have a toggle for enabling or disabling automatic sync. The ability to synchronize with other applications varies widely.

1. Launch the device's configuration menu.
2. To enable account syncing, go to Settings > Accounts > Google Account > About the Phone.
   - If your mobile device supports multiple user accounts, choose the one you want to access.
3. Check out a rundown of your synchronized Google applications and their last update times.

Look into other applications that may not have synced

Not all apps can automatically sync with your Google Account, so make sure you check the "Accounts" section of your phone's Settings app.

You may usually find a sign-in or sync option in the app's settings.

Disable The Sync Feature
Disable automatic updates for certain Google applications

1. Launch the device's configuration menu.
2. Check the Banks.
3. If your mobile device supports multiple accounts, choose the one you'd want to sync.
4. Select Account Sync from the menu.
5. Stop auto-syncing if there are any applications you don't want to.

Disabling automatic app updates does not uninstall the program itself. It only disables the app's incessant data updates.

Disable Google Account syncing immediately.

1. Launch the device's configuration menu.
2. To enable account syncing, go to Settings > Accounts > Google Account > About phone.
3. Disabling synchronization between items requires just a tap.

Sync Your Account Manually
1. Launch the device's configuration menu.
2. To enable account syncing, go to Settings > Accounts > Google Account > About the phone.
   - If your mobile device supports multiple accounts, choose the one you'd want to sync.
3. Simply choose 'More' and then 'Sync now' from the menu.

Even if auto-sync is off, a manual sync will update your account information across all of your Google applications.

Manage Your Pixel Apps
Apps may be removed, disabled, and managed on Android

Apps that have been installed on your phone may be removed. If you delete a premium app, you may always download it again in the future without having to pay again. The preinstalled applications on your phone may also be disabled.

Some of these instructions need Android 13 or later.

Erase Your Downloaded Programs
1. To access Google Play, launch the app.
2. Find the Profile button in the upper right corner.
3. Select Manage followed by Manage Apps & Devices.
4. To uninstall an app, choose it by tapping its name.
5. Select the Uninstall button.

An app may be reinstalled after being disabled or removed. You don't have to pay again to reinstall a program that you already purchased.

Turn Off The Default Applications
Some of the preloaded system applications on your Pixel phone cannot be removed. Most system applications, however, are turnable off.

1. Start the phone's configuration program.
2. The app you want to deactivate may be removed by selecting Apps, followed by All Apps.
3. You may turn it off by tapping the corresponding button up top.

The removal of any app from your Home screens is possible at any time.

Unused Software
Android will perform better after a lengthy period of non-use by doing the following:

- Making room by getting rid of old files
- Turning off app access
- Putting a halt to applications' background activity and notification sending

To go at previously underused but now optimized apps, click on Apps and then unused apps.

To disable this function for a single app, choose it from the list of candidates in App Info, then Unused applications, and finally excluded. If you're not using the app, this toggle should be turned off.

Establish A Screen Lock
Protect your Pixel by locking the screen

An Android device's screen may be locked for further protection. Your smartphone will need you to enter your unlock information (password, pattern, etc.) every time you use it. Fingerprint and face-unlocking features are available on various mobile devices.

- You'll need Android 10 or later to complete some of these procedures.
- You'll need to use touch input for a few of these tasks.

Adjust Screen Lock Settings

Use a PIN, pattern, or password to lock your screen and encrypt your automated and manual backups.

1. Start the phone's configuration program.
2. Lock it down.
3. Tap Screen Lock to choose a screen lock type.
    - To change locks once they have been established, you'll need to enter a PIN, pattern, or password.
4. Select the desired method of locking the screen. Just do what it says on the screen.
5. Next to "Screen lock," choose Settings to modify the parameters of your screen lock. The lock screen message, lock timer, and Power button lock may all be customized.

Safeguards For Your Screen
Deficiency of a lock

- No, your phone will not be locked again. While this provides no security, it does allow for a speedy return to the Home screen.
- Swipe: Move your finger horizontally across the display. While this provides no security, it does allow for a speedy return to the Home screen.

Normal Padlocks

- Create a basic pattern by tracing your finger over the page.
- Password: 4 digits or more are required. Generally speaking, longer PINs are safer.

- Enter a password of 4 digits or characters. The best way to protect your screen is with a complex password.

Increased Security Locks

- A fingerprint sensor allows you to use your unique print to unlock your phone.
- The Pixel 4, Pixel 7, and Pixel 7 Pro all include a facial recognition feature called Face Unlock.
- Leave your phone unlocked for longer while it's in particular locations, like your house.

By activating the lockdown, you may temporarily disable fingerprint unlocking and Smart Lock.

Using Your Fingerprint
Use your fingerprint to securely unlock your Pixel.

If your phone includes a fingerprint sensor, either on the display or the back, you may use it to unlock the device, make transactions, and get access to certain applications.

Please note that Android 9 or later is required for some of the instructions below.

Make Use Of Fingerprints
About the safety of fingerprints

To help keep your phone safe, we suggest always locking your screen. The fingerprint sensor on your phone is a quick and easy way to get access.

However, there are several things to remember:

- In certain cases, a password, pattern, or PIN is more secure than a fingerprint.
- Your phone might be unlocked using a replica of your fingerprint. Touching your phone leaves fingerprints on it, among other surfaces.
- You'll be prompted to provide a secondary password, pattern, or PIN. Keep in mind that there will be instances when you need to

resort to your backup, such as after a phone restart or when your fingerprint isn't detected.
- Up to five fingerprints may be stored.

Where Fingerprint Records Are Kept

Your fingerprint information is encrypted locally and never sent outside of your device. Not even Google or your phone's applications will have access to your information.

Create A Fingerprint System

To learn how to install Fingerprint Unlock on your Pixel phone, you may utilize the simulator.

If you have a Pixel 6 or later, you may use these instructions.

1. Launch the device's configuration menu.
2. Choose the Fingerprint Unlock option under Security.
3. Just do what it says on the screen. You will be prompted to set up a backup PIN, pattern, or password if you haven't previously done so.
4. Perform the first fingerprint scan.
    - Your phone's fingerprint reader is located towards the screen's bottom. The fingerprint sensor will light up and vibrate when you place your finger on the icon.
    - Put pressure on the display and keep it there. Put the middle of your finger on the sensor first. If you want your fingerprint's edges and tips captured, you'll need to move your finger as instructed.

If you have a Pixel 5a (5G) or a previous model, here's how to update:

1. Start the phone's configuration program.
2. Lock it down.
3. Try using Pixel Imprint.
4. Just do what it says on the screen. You will be prompted to set up a backup PIN, pattern, or password if you haven't previously done so.
5. Perform the first fingerprint scan.
    - Touch the sensor (not the display) on your phone.

- Keep your phone in the same hand position you use to unlock it. For instance, you should face the screen of your phone when using it.

If you add someone else's fingerprints to your phone, they will be able to access it and make purchases using your account. If you share your phone with others, they should use their accounts to add their fingerprints.

Put Your Fingerprint To Use
Phone, please unlock.

1. To unlock your phone, place your finger on the fingerprint sensor, which may be located on the front or back of your phone. Some smartphones need the power button to be pressed before the display will light up.

   To unlock your Pixel 6 or later phone, press and hold your fingerprint on the sensor for a few seconds.

2. For further safety, you may be required to switch to your secondary security PIN, pattern, or password on occasion. If:
   - After many attempts, your fingerprint still isn't being read.
   - To do this, you reset your device.
   - A new user is selected by you.
   - You haven't used your backup way of unlocking in more than 48 hours.

The fingerprint sensor will learn your fingerprint as you use it and become better and better. Your fingerprint scans are processed safely on your phone while you use it.

Allow purchases or unlock software

If you get a notification instructing you to scan your fingerprint, do so. Your fingerprint data is not sent to the app.

Modify Biometrics Preferences
Your fingerprints must be deleted or renamed.

1. Start the phone's configuration program.

2. Invoke the Help menu and then choose Security. Select between the Fingerprint or Pixel Imprint options.
3. Please scan your fingerprint, or use the other method of locking your screen.
4. Do what it is you want to do.
   - Select the fingerprint you want to remove, and then press the Delete button.
   - You may rename a fingerprint by selecting it, typing a new name, and then selecting OK.

Eliminate fingerprint use and remove them.

PIN, Pattern, Or Password Unlocking
One such unlocking method is to need a PIN, pattern, or password

If you want to utilize a PIN or pattern as a backup lock, you'll need to remove your fingerprint first.

1. Start the phone's configuration program.
2. Lock it down.
3. Select between the Fingerprint or Pixel Imprint options.
4. Put in your password, PIN, or fingerprint to get access.
5. Select Delete to get rid of a fingerprint. Do this again for each fingerprint.

Activating lockdown will temporarily disable fingerprint unlocking.

Disable The Phone's Screen Lock
The second choice is to disable the phone's screen lock.

For safety reasons, we insist that you keep your screen locked at all times. If you don't want to utilize a Smart Lock, fingerprint reader, PIN, pattern, or password, however:

1. Start the phone's configuration program.
2. Security System, After That Security lock.
3. Choose none or swipe left. Your fingerprints will be removed.

Fix Problems With Fingerprint

If you're having trouble using Fingerprint Unlock on your Pixel phone, you may follow a detailed guide on the Pixel phone simulator.

Pixel 6 and subsequent phones do not support fingerprint unlocking.

There are a few potential causes for your fingerprint not scanning:

Opening In The Direct Sunshine Of Day
Cover the fingerprint sensor and press and hold your fingertip firmly on it while scanning it outside in broad sunshine if you're having problems.

If Your Phone Is In Sleep Mode
If your phone is in sleep mode, you can't use the fingerprint scanner.

You may alter the settings so that the fingerprint sensor is always visible, even while the screen is off.

1. Gets the settings program going.
2. Lock the screen by selecting the Display menu.
3. Check the box next to Always display time and info.
   - You may also activate Tap to check the phone or Lift to check the phone to have easier access to the fingerprint sensor even while the phone is in a sleepy state.

Problems With The Screen Guard
The screen protector may be preventing your fingerprint from scanning. Always use a screen protector that has been approved by Google.

Problems with your fingerprint reader

If you're having problems, try these solutions:

- Update to the newest version of Android.
- Be careful to push down hard on the sensor and keep your finger there until the phone unlocks.
- Make sure the screen is free of fingerprints and other smudges. Make sure you are enrolling the same finger that you used to unlock the device. Follow the instructions to add a fingerprint, and you may use as many as five of them.
- Moisturize your fingers or enroll them again if they become too dry.

If none of this works, you'll need to un-enroll your fingerprint and enroll it again by going through the fingerprint setup process. When you re-enroll, take pictures of the sides and corners of your fingerprint as well.

Invalid fingerprints

If the fingerprint scanner does not recognize you:

- Get out your backup passcode and put it to use.
- Here's what you need to do to get into your phone if you've forgotten your backup password.

Once you're back in your phone, you may increase the likelihood that your fingerprint will be recognized:

1. Fingerprints may be altered.
2. When unlocking your phone, be sure you are holding it in the same manner you always have. For instance, you should face the screen of your phone when using it.
3. Put in as many as five fingerprints in case one of them is injured.

The screen lock was turned off

A new screen lock method may be required by your phone's administrator if you notice a "Screen locks option disabled" notification in the fingerprint settings. You may need to use a PIN, pattern, or password to access your work account on your phone, for instance. Your phone system administrator can make the necessary adjustments.

Fingerprint authorization for payments and app unlocking is still possible.

Face Unlocks Your Pixel
What makes Face Unlock tick

Pixel 4, Pixel 7, and Pixel 7 Pro users may make use of Face Unlock, which uses a 3D scan of your face to prove your identity. During setup, you will capture pictures of your face from various perspectives to use in creating the face model. Images of your face taken when using Face Unlock are utilized to refine your phone's facial recognition capabilities.

While we don't save the photos of your face that were used to make the model, we do keep the model itself in a safe place on your phone. Your phone does all the work in a safe environment.

If you sign up for Face Unlock, Google will only utilize the face model for that purpose, and it won't be shared with any other services or applications.

Follow the steps below for your specific Pixel phone model to remove your saved face model.

- Pixel 4, Pixel 4 XL, and Pixel 7
- In certain countries, face models may qualify as biometric data.
- You may accidentally unlock your phone just by looking at it.
- It's possible that Face Unlock isn't as safe as using a strong password or PIN.
- Someone who resembles you physically, such as an identical twin, may unlock your phone.
- Someone else can unlock your phone if they hold it up to your face. Don't take any chances by carrying your phone around with you.
- Face Unlock may fail if there isn't enough light or if you're wearing a mask or sunglasses. If you want a smoother unlocking experience, you should also sign up for Fingerprint Unlock.

Pixel 7 and Pixel 7 Plus

You may use Face Unlock to access your Pixel 7 or Pixel 7 Pro.

The Pixel 7 and Pixel 7 Pro do not support the usage of Face Unlock for logging into applications or making purchases. Fingerprint Unlock and/or robust passwords, patterns, and PINs may be used instead for these tasks.

Configure Face Unlock

1. Launch the Pixel's settings menu.
2. To enable Face & Fingerprint Unlock, go to Settings > Security.
3. Put in the code or password.

4. Select "Face Unlock," "I Agree," and "Start" from the on-screen prompts.
5. Tap the Done button after completing the on-screen prompts.

Modify your Face Unlock preferences

Cast Off The Lock-Up

You may activate the Skip lock screen to bypass the first unlocking process and go straight to your previously used screen.

When using Face Unlock, you can:

1. Launch the Pixel's settings menu.
2. To enable Face & Fingerprint Unlock, go to Settings > Security.
3. Put in the code or password.
4. Method: Use the Face Unlock button.
5. Just disable the screen lock.

Purge Facial Records

It is possible to erase face data to remove your face model or disable Face Unlock.

When using Face Unlock, you can:

1. Launch the Pixel's settings menu.
2. To enable Face & Fingerprint Unlock, go to Settings > Security.
3. Put in the code or password.
4. Method: Use the Face Unlock button.
5. Select the Face Model you want to remove, and then tap Delete.

Have One's Eyes Open

"Require eyes to be open" is turned on automatically. You may disable this function for Face Unlock if you want to be able to unlock your phone with your eyes closed.

When using Face Unlock, you can:

1. Launch the device's configuration menu.
2. To enable Face & Fingerprint Unlock, go to Settings > Security.
3. Put in the code or password.
4. Method: Use the Face Unlock button.

5. Select "When Using Face Unlock," and then disable Needs awake eyes.

Improve the reliability of Face Unlock

Face Unlock's Facial Recognition
My problems with Face Unlock's facial recognition

1. Verify that you have fingerprint and facial recognition set up to unlock your smartphone.
   - Launch the Pixel's settings menu.
   - To enable Face & Fingerprint Unlock, go to Settings > Security.
   - Put in the code or password.
2. Make sure you're not in a place with very little light, like a cave.
3. Take off any masks or sunglasses that could be getting in the way, and give it another go.
4. Make sure that your default look is saved in Face Unlock. Whether you wear glasses, a headscarf, or no makeup at all is one illustration of this. Your face may be re-enrolled if there has been a major change in your look.

Too many times has Face Unlock been activated

Both the "Tap to check phone" and the "Lift to check phone" options are turned on by default. You may disable these features to lessen the likelihood that your phone will unlock on its own. When these settings are disabled, Face Unlock cannot be activated until the screen is woken up by pressing the power button.

The Face Unlock Feature Does Not Activate

1. Double-check that both "Tap to check phone" and "Lift to check phone" are enabled.
2. To check whether the face scanner is active, tap the screen and look for a moving circle or other animation around the camera.
3. Make sure you've activated Face & Fingerprint Unlock:
   1. Launch the Pixel's settings menu.
   2. To enable Face & Fingerprint Unlock, go to Settings > Security.
   3. Put in the code or password.

4. In "Unlock Methods," the option to "Unlock with Face" has been introduced.
5. Make sure the switch for Unlock is engaged.

Schedule Your Pixel Phone
Schedule When Your Pixel Will Remain Unlocked.

Your Pixel phone does not need to be locked while it is in your pocket or when it is synced with another device you use often. Smart Lock simply requires you to enter your PIN, pattern, or password into the lock once. The capabilities of your gadget will determine what you can do.

- You'll need Android 10 or later to complete some of these procedures.
- You'll need to use touch input for a few of these tasks.

Don't Lock Your Phone
1. Set up a password on your screen.
2. Start the phone's configuration program.
3. Select Security, then More Options. Smart Lock comes next.
4. Put in the code or password.
5. Select a choice and carry out the instructions shown.

Turning on the screen after having unlocked the phone will reveal a pulsating circle around the Lock, indicating that the phone is still unlocked. After 4 hours of inactivity, your phone will restart and need unlocking.

To relock your device, tap and hold the Lock icon.

Stop Using The Smart Lock
1. Start the phone's configuration program.
2. Select Smart Lock by going to the Security > Advanced Settings menu.
3. Put in the code or password.
4. Try out the on-body scanner.
5. Do not make use of on-body detection.
6. Take away any safe havens. Optional.

Find Your Locking Choices

Turning on Smart Lock secures your mobile device.

Lock the phone even when the feature is set to unlock automatically.

1. To unlock your phone, just press the Unlock button.
   - Accessibility mode TalkBack is activated by tapping Unlock twice.
2. The lock will remain in effect until you unlock the phone with your password, pattern, or fingerprint again.

Use Find My Device to lock your phone from a distance.

Your phone may be locked from a distance using a computer, tablet, or another smartphone.

Don't go about with your phone locked.

Body detection may be toggled on and off.

1. Choose On-body detection from Smart Lock's menu.
2. Set the body detection mode to on or off.

Methods Of On-Person Detection
- Once your phone is unlocked, it will remain unlocked as long as it is close to your body. If you put your phone down, say on a table, it may take up to a minute to lock itself.
- The on-body detection feature of certain smartphones can analyze your gait and adapt to it. Your phone might be locked if it detects a highly unusual gait. If your phone locks up after you take a walk, all you have to do is unlock it, and it will pick up on the differences in your gait.
- It may take your phone 5-10 minutes to lock once you enter a moving vehicle (a car, bus, train, etc.).
- Remember that your phone may not automatically lock when you're in the air or on the water. If you need to manually lock, do so.

You can tell when you're carrying your phone with you by looking at the accelerometer data it has stored about your walking habits.

Turning off on-body detection causes your phone to erase this information.

In safe environments, you should always leave your phone unlocked.

Seek Reliable Sources

- Give your phone permission to utilize your location.
- Wi-Fi is recommended for secure locations.

The location you have trusted is just an approximation.

Your reliable spot isn't limited to the confines of your house or other personal space. Within a range of up to 80 meters, it will maintain your phone's unlocked status.

It is possible to intercept and alter location signals. Your phone might be unlocked by someone with the right tools.

Put an end to the lock screen notifications.

Switch To Lockdown
Lockdown will only prevent access to your phone till you open it. You'll need to manually activate the lockdown every time you wish to utilize it.

1. Keep your finger on the power button for a few seconds.
2. Turn on the locks. While in lock screen mode, this disables all alerts, fingerprint/face unlocking, and Smart Lock.

When linked to a safe device, leave the lock unlocked.

Put in a reliable Bluetooth gadget.

1. Verify that Bluetooth is enabled on your device.
2. Start the phone's configuration program.
3. Select Smart Lock by going via the Security > Advanced settings menu.
4. Input Credible Equipment, and then include reliable hardware.
5. Select a gadget from the list and tap it.
   - When paired with a reliable accessory, such as a Bluetooth watch or in-car audio system, you may leave your phone

unlocked for extended periods. Always-connected accessories, such as Bluetooth keyboards and phone covers, should be avoided.
6. Optional: Simply tapping the desired Bluetooth device will delete it. Then, choose Device Forget from the menu.
7. Please unlock your phone. If you keep your phone linked to the approved gadget, it will remain unlocked.

Make sure your trusted Bluetooth gadgets are safe.

Someone may fake your Bluetooth connection and use it to keep your phone unlocked.

When your phone is unable to verify that you are connected over a secure channel, it will alert you. Your phone may need unlocking.

The effective range of Bluetooth connections varies. Your phone's model, the Bluetooth device you're using, and the surrounding conditions all affect range. The maximum range for a Bluetooth connection is 100 meters. Someone may get access to your phone if they stole it while it was in proximity to your trusted device and it had unlocked it.

Protect Your Electronic Gadgets

Passwords stored in your Google Account may be used across many devices when you do one of the following:

- Chrome on Android: Activate Sync
- Launch Google Chrome and log in.

Google's Password Storage

When you log in to a website or app using Android or Chrome, you will be offered to store your password if you have the option to do so enable.

Click Save to permanently save your password for the app or website. You may choose which of your signed-in Google Accounts on your Android smartphone to save the password.

Your stored passwords are always accessible in Chrome or on passwords.google.com.

Managing Your Passwords

Chrome may sign you in automatically to sites using the login information stored in your Google Account.

You may toggle the "Offer to save passwords" setting, which is enabled by default.

1. Launch Chrome on your laptop.
2. To access your passwords, click Profile Profile in the upper right corner.
   - If you can't locate the Passwords icon, try clicking More Organize in the upper right, followed by Settings, Autofill, and finally Password Manager.
3. Change the setting for the password-saving offer.

Handle Requests To Remember
Handle requests to remember passwords for individual services.

Passwords for individual websites may be disabled in this way. Never choose to store a password when requested to do so. There will be no prompt to store the password in the future.

Password-saving options for the following sites may be seen or changed here:

1. Launch Chrome on your laptop.
2. To access your passwords, click Profile Profile in the upper right corner.
   - If you can't locate the Passwords icon, try clicking More Organize in the upper right, followed by Settings, Autofill, and finally Password Manager.
3. In the section labeled "Never Saved," you'll see a list of all the sites that will never prompt you to store your password. Click the delete button to get rid of a site.

Control Automatic Logins

Using previously entered information; you may instantly access your favorite sites and applications. You may disable automatic sign-in if you want to be prompted for confirmation each time you log in.

1. Launch Chrome on your laptop.
2. To access your passwords, click Profile Profile in the upper right corner.
    - If you can't locate the Passwords icon, try clicking More Organize in the upper right, followed by Settings, Autofill, and finally Password Manager.
3. Flip the switch for automatic sign-in.

Locate A Lost Gadget
If you lose your Pixel, you better have a plan.

You can make sure Find My Device can locate your phone in case you ever misplace it.

Android 8.0 or later is required for some of the instructions below.

Locate Your Gadgets
See to it that your gadget can be located.

If you're looking for an Android smartphone, try to zero down on one that:

- Currently logged on their Google Account
- Is the Location on and working?
- Are you using Find My Device?
- Is charged and linked to a network through mobile data or WiFi.
- You can still access your device's last known position, even if it's turned off or disconnected from a network, by toggling on "Store recent location."
- Appear in the Google Play store

To lock or wipe data from an Android smartphone, you must first:

- Quite potent
- Uses wireless or cellular data
- Has Find My Device enabled Is logged into a Google account
- Appear in the Google Play store

Make sure you're logged in to a Google Account.

1. Launch the device's configuration menu.
2. Tap your profile picture in the upper right corner.
3. Check that you entered the proper email address when you signed in.

Verify that the Location is turned on

1. Launch the device's configuration menu.
2. Find Your Spot.
3. Get Location turned on.

Make sure Find My Device is turned on

Devices that have been hidden via Google Play will not appear in the app.

1. Launch the device's configuration menu.
2. Choose the Find My Device option under Security.
   - To access "Security," try tapping Security & Location or Google And then Security.
3. Verify that "Find My Device" is on.

Make sure you can locate your gadget.

A device that has been hidden in Google Play will not be visible in Find My Device.

1. Launch Google Play and go to its Library > Devices page.
2. Check the "Show In Menus" box in the upper left corner.

Get The App

Install the Find My Device app on one Android phone or tablet so you're ready to use it to locate another.

Recover A Misplaced Pixel Phone

Recover a misplaced Pixel phone, lock it, or wipe its contents.

Your phone may be tracked down, locked, or deleted if you misplace it. After linking your phone to your Google Account, Find My Device will be enabled.

If you're looking for an Android smartphone, try to zero down on one that:

- Currently logged on their Google Account
- Is the Location on and working?
- Are you using Find My Device?
- Is charged and linked to a network through mobile data or WiFi.
- You can still access your device's last known position, even if it's turned off or disconnected from a network, by toggling on "Store recent location."
- Appear in the Google Play store

To lock or wipe data from an Android smartphone, you must first:

- Quite potent
- Uses wireless or cellular data
- Currently logged on their Google Account
- Are you using Find My Device?
- Appear in the Google Play store

Remotely Locate A Device
Remotely locate, lock, or delete a device

1. Use your browser to visit android.com/find.
2. Log in using your Google credentials.
   - If you own many electronic gadgets: Choose the misplaced gadget from the list at the top of the sidebar.
   - If the missing gadget has more than one user account: Use your primary or personal Google Account to sign in.
3. A message is sent to the misplaced gadget.
4. You can see the device's location on a map.
   - This may not be an exact description of the area.
   - If your gadget is missing, its last known location may be revealed.
5. Select "Enable lock & erase" if prompted to do so.
6. Choose your preferred action:
   - Activate audio: It will ring your phone for 5 minutes straight, regardless of its current volume setting.
   - Safe gadget: Uses a password or PIN to secure the device. A lock may be established even if none is present. Leaving a

note or the device number on the lock screen might help someone find your lost gadget and return it to you.
- Wipe memory: Deletes information from your device permanently, but may not remove SD cards. Once you've erased your device, Find My Device wills no longer function.

If you've synced your phone with Google, you can use the "find my phone" feature on google.com to locate or ring it.

Try the Find My Device app.

1. Launch the Find My Device app from a different Android phone or tablet.
   - You can acquire the app from Google Play if the other gadget doesn't already have it.
2. Do so here.
   - Click Continue as [your name] if you don't have access to your device.
   - You may assist a friend sign-in by selecting the "Sign in as guest" option.
3. Choose the gadget you're trying to track down from the list provided.
   - The same choices are presented in both sets of instructions.
4. You may be asked to enter the passcode for the locked screen of the Android smartphone you're trying to track down. All versions of Android 9 and above are supported. If the lost smartphone doesn't have a PIN and is running Android 8 or earlier, you may be asked to enter your Google password.
5. To remotely locate, lock, or delete a device, just repeat the previous procedures.

Use your Wear OS watch to locate your mobile device.

Wear OS smartwatches may be used to track down a misplaced Android smartphone or tablet.

Wireless Charge Your Devices
Pixel Stands allow for wireless charging of mobile devices.

Phones that have the Qi certification may be charged with your Pixel Stand. While you're Pixel 3, Pixel 4, Pixel 5, Pixel 6, Pixel 6

Pro, Pixel 7, or Pixel 7 Pro is charging on the Pixel Stand, you can also use Google Assistant to get some work done.

Power For Charging

The second-generation Pixel Stand supports quick wireless charging at speeds of up to:

Pixel 7 Pro or Pixel 6 Pro (additional steps needed)	23W
Pixel 7 (additional steps needed)	20W
Pixel 6 (additional steps needed)	21W
Pixel 3/3 XL, Pixel 4/4 XL, or Pixel 5	10W
Other Qi-compatible devices	15W

Different gadgets that may use QiThe Pixel Buds and other Qi-compatible earbuds may be charged wirelessly by using the 15W Pixel Stand.

The original Pixel Stand supports wireless charging speeds of up to:

- 10W for all Pixel phones that can use it
- 5W for devices that are Qi-compatible

The actual time it takes to charge a smartphone is affected by several variables, including the device's battery life and whether or not a protective cover is being used.

Activate Rapid Charging

You may charge your Pixel 7 Pro or Pixel 6 Pro at up to 23W, your Pixel 7 at up to 20W, and your Pixel 6 at up to 21W if you do the following:

1. Verify that you are running the most recent software version on your phone. Later software updates will allow for fast wireless charging of up to 23W, as shown in SQ1D.211205.016.A1 and SQ1D.220105.007.
2. Finish the app tutorial for Pixel Stand.

After updating your Pixel phone's firmware and setting up the Pixel Stand app, you'll be able to charge wirelessly at up to 23W while also making use of the Pixel Stand's unique Fan Controls, Photo Frames, and Immersive Media features.

Display Stand Requirements

Pixel Stand-compatible phones

In addition to the Pixel 4, Pixel 5, Pixel 6, Pixel 6 Pro, Pixel 7, and Pixel 7 Pro, you may use your Pixel Stand to charge any Qi wireless charging compatible device.

Check the phone's technical specifications or get in touch with the maker to find out whether Qi wireless charging is supported.

Compatible Pixel Stand cases

Most phone covers up to 3 mm in thickness will not prevent your Pixel Stand from charging your phone. Here are several examples:

- Most Google Pixel cases are made by Google.
- Google's Pixel 3: My Argument

Your phone's charging speed (or lack thereof) may be affected by the material from which its cover is constructed.

Cases with metal, batteries, or accessories like mounts and grips will prevent your Pixel Stand from charging your phone.

Create A Stand For Your Pixel

Make sure you have the Pixel Stand's included power adapter and USB-C cable (1.5 meters in length).

1. Connect one end of the cable to the Pixel Stand's USB-C connector (located on the base of the stand).
2. Connect the cord's opposite end to the power supply.
3. Connect the power adapter to an electrical outlet.

If you're not using the power adapter that comes with your Pixel Stand, you may only be able to charge at 5W. A 30W USB PD power adapter that supports a minimum of 14V, such as the adapter included with your Pixel Stand (2nd gen), is required for high-power charging (up to 23W on Pixel 7 Pro and Pixel 6 Pro).

Put your electronic devices on charge

You may start charging your phone or headphones immediately after setting up your Pixel Stand.

The Pixel phone may only be charged when standing up in portrait mode on the Pixel Stand (second generation).

Position your phone so that the screen is facing outward on the Pixel Stand.

Earphone charging instructions:

1. Get your headphones out of your bag.
2. Put the Pixel Stand in the middle of your case.

Pixel Stand LED Patterns

The Pixel Stand has several LED patterns that indicate the health of your smartphone.

The white light

A white light will illuminate for around 4 seconds while a smartphone is charging in the Pixel Stand or when the battery is at 100%.

Amber glow (original Pixel Stand only).

Something is blocking the charging process, or the gadget isn't in the right spot. This problem may be resolved by:

- Change where your phone is sitting on the stand.
- Take your phone out of its cover. Do it again if necessary.
- De-metalize your phone by removing any metallic stickers. Do it again if necessary.

(Only on the second-generation Pixel Stand) A flashing white and amber light.

Something is blocking the charging process, or the gadget isn't in the right spot. This problem may be resolved by:

- Change where your phone is sitting on the stand.
- Take your phone out of its cover. Do it again if necessary.
- De-metalize your phone by removing any metallic stickers. Do it again if necessary.

Amber light blinks slowly.

Every two seconds or so, an amber light will flash. The dock isn't designed to work with the power supply you're using. To charge your phone with the Pixel Stand (2nd gen), you'll need a power adapter with a 12W rating or greater.

- If you're using the Pixel Stand's included power supply, try unplugging it and then plugging it back in.
- If you are not using the power adaptor that comes with your Pixel Stand, try using it instead.

If you're not using the power adapter that comes with your Pixel Stand, you may only be able to charge at 5W. A 30W USB PD power adapter that supports a minimum of 14V, such as the adapter included with your Pixel Stand (2nd gen), is required for high-power charging (up to 23W on Pixel 7 Pro and Pixel 6 Pro).

Pixel Phone customer service should be contacted if any unusual LED patterns are seen.

Get Services Of Google Assistant
Help yourself to the services of Google Assistant on your Pixel 3, Pixel 4, Pixel 5, Pixel 6, Pixel 6 Pro, Pixel 7, or Pixel 7 Pro.

While your Pixel 3, Pixel 4, Pixel 5, Pixel 6, Pixel 6 Pro, Pixel 7, or Pixel 7 Pro is charging on the Pixel Stand, you may use Google Assistant to get some work done.

Set Up Your Pixel Stand
You and your assistant will set up your Pixel stand.

1. Position your phone so that the screen is facing outward on the Pixel Stand.
2. A "Do more while charging" notification will show up. Select the Next button.
   - If you are not seeing this prompt, remove your phone from the Pixel Stand and reattach it.
   - If you are still unable to locate this notification, please check your phone's Settings > Connected Devices menu. Select Pixel Stand > Settings from the menu.
3. Just do what it says on the screen.

Activate Individual Outcomes
Google Assistant can help you keep track of things like appointments, reminders, and email. This data is also available on the unlocked screen of your phone.

To see your information, you must activate personal results.

modify your Pixel Stand's Assistant preferences.

1. Start the phone's configuration program.
2. Pick the gadgets that are linked.
3. A "Pixel Stand" entry should appear under "Previously connected devices," but if not, choose to See All.
4. Select Pixel Stand > Settings from the menu.
5. Select the picture frame by tapping on it.
6. Activate or deactivate the Assistant features:
   - Results from my use of Pixel Stand: While your phone is resting on the Pixel Stand, you can get your personalized results even if the screen is locked.
   - Use your phone's ambient display while it's charging to show your unique stats. Activate the background image.
   - Use your Pixel Stand as a picture frame with an ambient display to show off your favorite Google Photos. Simply choose the picture frame icon on the background screen. Select Google Photos albums to pick from a collection of images. From the lock screen, slide right to access the photo frame.

Modify Charging Settings
Modify Pixel Stand (second generation) charging settings.

If you've previously set up the Pixel Stand app, you have three options for charging:

- The default setting, "optimized," strikes a good balance between charging speed and fan noise right out of the box.
- Maximal: The fastest charging speed achievable for the gadget and the battery.
- Keeps the fan running at a whisper.

Pixel Stand (2nd gen) default mode selection:

1. Launch the device's configuration menu.
2. Pick the gadgets that are linked.
3. If "Pixel Stand Gen 2" isn't shown under "Previous devices connected," choose to See All.
4. Select "Pixel Stand Gen 2" from the "Other devices" menu.
5. Select "Charging mode" from the list of options on the "Device Details" screen.
6. Choose a power source by pressing the appropriate button.

To switch gears momentarily:

1. The phone must be placed on the stand.
2. The Pixel Stand Control Screen may be accessed by tapping the screen.
3. Select a charging method from the drop-down menu.

The Pixel Stand's default charging mode will be used the next time it is used. The button will display the accent color of the phone when the setting is activated by a tap or made persistently.

Modify Screen Brightness

Pixel 3, Pixel 4, Pixel 5, Pixel 6, Pixel 6 Pro, Pixel 7, and Pixel 7 Pro): Modify notifications and screen brightness.

1. Launch the device's configuration menu.
2. Pick the gadgets that are linked.
3. A "Pixel Stand" entry should appear under "Previously connected devices," but if not, choose to See All.
4. Select Pixel Stand > Settings from the menu.
5. Toggle the on/off switch:

- Turn off the TV at night: Turn off your phone's display while you're in a dark place.
- When docked, please do not disturb: While your phone is charging, you may mute any alerts you might get.
- Display pictures from Google Photos on a frame while your phone is propped up in the Pixel Stand. Simply choose the picture frame icon on the background screen. Select Google Photos albums to pick from a collection of images.
- The 15 minutes before your alarm, have your phone's screen gradually brighten up to simulate a sunrise. The time frame is flexible.
- If you have a bedtime routine in place, you will get a notice when it is time for bed. To activate your alarm and begin your night's rest: Select the desired sleep noise or "Going to sleep" from the alert's menu. Change the tune.

Repair Your Pixel Stand

No wireless charging for the phone

You should test your charger after applying each of the following fixes to see whether it has begun charging.

- Remove the cover and any other add-ons, such as the mount and the grip.
- Make sure the front of your phone is facing away from the Pixel Stand and the back is resting against it.
- Put the Pixel on the stand's center.
- It's worth a shot to try charging your phone both vertically and horizontally.
- To power your Pixel Stand, plug it in using the cord and adapter that came with it.
- Verify that both the power adapter and the cable are connected to a functional power source.

On the bottom, an orange light glows.

There seems to be an issue with charging your phone using the Pixel Stand. After completing each of the steps below, make sure your charger is up and running.

- Take your phone out of the Pixel Stand and replace it.
- Place your phone on the Pixel Stand so that it is dead center.
- It's worth a shot to try charging your phone both vertically and horizontally.
- Remove the cover from your phone and replace it on the Pixel Stand.

The Pixel or Phone Dock is Hot to the Touch

While charging, it's natural for your phone and the Pixel Stand to become somewhat warmer than usual. Neither your Pixel phone nor Pixel Stand should become too hot when charging.

You may notice that your phone or Pixel Stand is warmer than usual while charging from a low battery.

This Pixel Stand is a Mess

1. Take the Pixel Stand off your phone.
2. Disconnect the Pixel Stand's cord.
3. Wipe the area down carefully using isopropyl alcohol (IPA) wipes.
4. Once your phone is dry, you may return it to the Pixel Stand.

With TalkBack on, I am unable to access the Pixel Stand settings.

The Pixel Stand settings symbol will appear in the upper right corner of your phone's screen for the first 15 seconds while charging. The Pixel Stand settings icon vanishes after 15 seconds.

To access the TalkBack options in Pixel Stand:

1. Double-tap the screen once with your fingers.
2. Double-tap anywhere on the screen after swiping or exploring with one finger to access the Pixel Stand's configuration options.

Chapter Seven
Manage Pixel Phone Alerts

You may adjust your phone's global settings or those of individual applications to get the alerts you desire. Swiping down from the top of the screen brings up the notification drawer. The lock screen and home screen may also display some notifications.

Some of these instructions need Android 11 or later.

Make Use Of Alerts

Do Not Disturb can silence alerts. Practice using the "Do Not Disturb" feature.

Discernible Alerts

- Swipe left or right to dismiss the selected alert.
- Scroll down to the very bottom of your alerts and choose Clear All to delete them all at once.
- Next to "silent notifications," choose Close to dismiss any pending alerts.

Some alerts may be dismissed only when their associated tasks have been completed. When you pause your music player, the notice disappears.

Reminders to wake up

Activate The Nap Mode
1. Select "Settings" from your phone's menu.
2. Select "Alerts" from the menu.
3. Enable the option to snooze notifications.

Put A Message On Hold
Simply swipe a notification to the left or right and release it to snooze it. Select a time slot by using the Down arrow.

Easily communicate, organize, and grow

- Tap the Down arrow to open a notice. Then, choose an option from the notice itself, such as Reply or Archive, to take immediate action.

- When you get a notice, certain applications will display a dot. To see the most recent notification, touch and hold the app that has the dot. Finally, wipe the slate clean to reveal the following step.

Display both active and dormant alerts

After dismissing or pausing a notice, it will remain in your device's notification history for further review.

1. Start the phone's configuration program.
2. To see past alerts, go to Settings > Notifications.
3. Change the setting for Notification history use.

Manage Mass Notifications in Case of Emergencies

Sound and vibration may be adjusted, and you can enable or disable different sorts of notifications.

1. Launch the phone's Settings menu.
2. Select Alerts, then. Notifications in the event of an emergency may now be sent wirelessly.
3. Decide how frequently you want to be notified and what options you want to activate.

Pick Your Method Of Alert
Modify your phone's alert settings.

1. Start the phone's configuration program.
2. Select Alerts, then. Lock-screen alerts for messages.
   - Set the alert preferences on your phone:
   - Demonstrate talk, default, and no sound.
   - Conceal notifiable discussions and silence
   - Don't display any alerts
   - Under "General," you may toggle the following additional alerts on and off:
   - Cover the status bar's silence with sound
   - The in-app notification dot must support snoozing.
   - Improvements to Alert Systems

The screen of certain phones may be set to automatically turn on whenever you get a notice. Find out how to activate the ambient screen.

App-specific notification controls

Access The Settings Menu
1. Start the phone's configuration program.
2. Choose App settings by tapping Notifications.
3. Look under "Most recent" to see which programs have lately notified you of anything.
   - Select All applications from the aforementioned menu to explore other options.
4. Simply use the app by tapping on it.
5. Modify the app's notification settings as needed.
   - If an app is on the list, you may disable its notifications entirely.
   - Select which kind of alerts the app should send you by tapping on its name.

In Response To An Alert
1. From the top of your screen, slide down to access your phone's notification menu.
2. To change the settings, touch and hold the alert.
3. Make some selections:
   - Disabling All notifications will disable all alerts.
   - Modify your notification settings as needed.
   - Simply activate the toggle for "Allow notification dot" to enable the dots.

Within This One App
Many app alerts may be changed from inside the app's settings menu. For instance, some apps may allow you to choose the music that plays when you get a notice from the app. Launch the program and look for an option to tweak the parameters.

Toggle the status dots on and off

1. Start the phone's configuration program.
2. Select "Alerts" from the menu.
3. Toggle the app's notification icon dot on and off.

Decide Whether To Be Notified
You may decide whether or not to be bothered with alerts.

It's up to you to decide how an app should notify you:

- Sound will play, a message will appear on your lock screen, and an app's icon will appear in the status bar to alert you.
- No noise or vibrations will be produced or felt. However, you'll only see the alert if you swipe down from the top of the screen.

Access The Settings Menu
1. Start the phone's configuration program.
2. Select Alerts, and then Configuration options for the app.
3. Look under "Most recent" to see which programs have lately notified you of anything.
   - Select All applications from the aforementioned menu to explore other options.
4. Simply use the app by tapping on it.
5. Select a notification type by tapping its icon.
6. Pick one of these. You may toggle on or off several sorts of alerts across applications.

In Response To An Alert
1. Swipe down from where you are now.
2. Keep holding the alert on your screen.
3. Choose Ignore or Silent Mode.
4. Click the "Apply" button.

Set The Bubble Intensity
1. Launch the device's configuration menu.
2. Select Bubbles from the Notifications menu.
3. Enable the App's bubble display setting.

Toggle Bubbles On Or Off
You may toggle bubbles on or off for individual programs and conversations.

1. Launch the device's configuration menu.
2. Mobile Apps.
3. Select the option to View All Apps. Then, choose the app you want to modify and press it.

4. Select Alerts, then. Additional app preferences, followed by the Bubbles feature.
5. Pick your alert preferences:
   - Everyone is free to speak their opinions.
   - Some discussions may be bubbled up: Just tap someone on the shoulder. Activate Bubble after that.
   - There will be no bubbling.

Manage How Alerts Appear
Modify how alerts appear behind the lock screen.

If you make this your default setting, it will affect all applications going forward.

1. Start the phone's configuration program.
2. Select Apps & Notifications > Notifications.
3. On the locked screen, choose Notifications.
4. Take your pick:
   - Display Talking, Default, and Silent Modes: Put all alerts right on the locked screen.
   - Cover up your phone's alerts and quiet conversations: The lock screen should show notifications.
   - Do not display alerts: On the lock screen, disable all alerts. Only when the user unlocks their phone will they get alerts?

Display Private Information
Use a lock screen to display private information.

1. Start the phone's configuration program.
2. Select "Alerts" from the menu.
3. Under "Privacy," toggle the switch for "Sensitive" alerts.

Tip: you can still set individual applications to "Don't show notifications" on the lock screen even if you disable this feature.

Reduce Distractions
The Pixel phone's Do Not Disturb mode might help you reduce distractions.

Do Not Disturb is a feature that mutes your phone. This setting may muffle audio, disable vibration, and obscure your view. You have control over what is blocked and what is allowed.

Some of these instructions need Android 11 or later.

Quickly Toggle Interruptions
You can quickly mute or play-back interruptions.

Here are a few suggestions for turning off your phone:

- To the whole family of Pixel devices: Swipe down from the top of the screen. After that, choose the "Do Not Disturb" option.
- For Pixel 2, 3, and 4: Squeezing your phone will put an end to any incoming calls.
- Phones with a Pixel 2 or later should be placed flat with the display facing up.
- From a different source: You may instruct your Smart Display or speaker to muffle your phone's volume.

Modify Your Alert Preferences
Decide what to obstruct

1. Start the phone's configuration program.
2. A tappable, vibrating sound And then, please, do not disturb.
3. Find the setting for "What can interrupt Do Not Disturb?" and toggle it on or off as needed.
    - People, please disable or enable phone calls, texts, and chats.
    - Apps: Select which ones may give you alerts.
    - Interruptions like alarms, media, touch noises, reminders, and calendar events may be muted or turned on.

Important alerts will appear regardless of your notification settings, so don't worry about that. For instance, security alerts from the system cannot be disabled.

Limit who may talk over your pauses

1. Start the phone's configuration program.
2. A tappable, vibrating sound This was followed by the Keep Peace!

3. Select People under "What can interrupt Do Not Disturb?"
4. Pick what you'll let through:
   - Talks: any talks
   - Crucial communications. Tap Settings to choose your preferred chats as your top priority.
   - No One Calls: Everyone in your address book or favorites
   - Persistent callers. Turn on Allow repeat callers to allow calls through from the same number again within 15 minutes.
   - Anyone, your contacts, or your favorite contacts
   - None Reminders
   - Events

Your "starred" contacts will always appear at the top of the Contacts list. Discover how to save people as favorites.

Timeouts may be customized.

1. Start the phone's configuration program.
2. To disable alerts and vibrations, press the Do Not Disturb button. Timeout in Quick Preferences.
3. You may customize the duration of the Do Not Disturb mode.
   - Until it is turned off
   - For a certain amount of time, say, two hours or fifteen minutes.
   - Constantly inquire
4. Tap OK.

Modify the parameters for discreet alerts

1. Start the phone's configuration program.
2. To turn this feature off, choose Do Not Disturb from the menu under Sound & Vibration.
3. For discreet alerts, go to the Display settings menu.
4. Pick and choose which content to restrict or allow:
   - If you disable this feature, alerts will still appear, but no sound will play.
   - Disabling this option will prevent any alerts from appearing on your screen or playing any sounds.

- Personalized: You may change the appearance of the on-screen notification dots and the behavior of the off-screen blink light.

Automatically Halt Disruptions

When your Google Calendar is full of activities and appointments

1. Start the phone's configuration program.
2. Select Schedules from the Sound & Vibration menu.
3. Select a timetable from the available options. To make adjustments, you may either touch the timetable or the Settings button.
   - You may choose the days on which Do Not Disturb will activate while you sleep, for instance.
4. Select the Add More button to create a new rule.
5. Select a Time or Event.
6. Change the name, activation time, and other settings for your rule.
7. Make sure the rule is turned on at the very top.
   - Select Delete to get rid of a rule.

Before sleeping ("bedtime mode")

Bedtime mode allows you to set your phone to automatically enter Do Not Disturb mode whenever you're about to stop using it, such as when you go to sleep.

- Do Not Disturb and Android Auto are both safe to use while driving with a Pixel 3 or later. Get schooled on the different driving modes.
- Pixel 2: When driving, you may activate the Do Not Disturb mode.

Engage With Your Applications
Engage with your environment and the applications in it.

Your phone is a great tool for meeting and talking to people in your immediate area. Apps that support nearby allow you to do things like play games or collaborate with pals.

- You'll need Android 10 or later to complete some of these procedures.
- You'll need to use touch input for a few of these tasks.

Needed Items

To engage in conversation:

- You can't be more than 30 meters (around 100 feet) away.
- To communicate with others, you and they must use the same app.
- You can't work together in an app that doesn't support Nearby.

The Process Of Nearby

Apps that support nearby will prompt users close to asking whether they want to connect when they both have the same app open.

The Nearby app connects to Google and retrieves information on jointly used apps using minimal quantities of Wi-Fi or mobile bandwidth.

Nearby does not collect or transmit any information about you or your phone. Apps that support nearby may communicate with one another over third-party servers when permitted to do so. There is no direct connection between the sharing devices.

See what programs are compatible with Nearby.

1. Launch the device's configuration menu.
2. Select the Privacy menu, followed by the Privacy settings panel. This was followed by the Check with other authorizations.
3. Use the gadgets close by.
4. Tap the app to disable its Nearby alerts. Scroll down until you see "Nearby devices access for this app," and then choose "Don't allow."

You can disable nearby notifications without affecting the functionality of an app, so don't worry.

To troubleshoot, verify all connections and settings.

Bluetooth and Placement

- You must have both Bluetooth and Location enabled to get nearby alerts.
- Your phone will prompt you to enable Bluetooth or Location if you allow an app to utilize nearby while they are disabled.

Connectivity issues? Try another network

- Make sure your mobile device is online so you can get Nearby alerts.

Printed in Great Britain
by Amazon